ENDORSEMENTS

Joseph Z's newest book *Punishing the Darkness* is a one-of-a-kind book that you will devour from the moment you set your eyes on it. It is unquestionably the most unique book I've ever read on spiritual warfare, and it covers an array of topics on this subject combined in a way I've never seen before in a single volume. We are living in times when it seems the veil between the spirit world, *both good and evil spiritual forces*, and the natural world is getting thinner, and we are becoming increasingly more aware of these two very different worlds and how they influence each other. As an endorser, I read this book from cover to cover, and I found myself captivated and challenged as I read it. This is a book for overcomers—it speaks to wherever you are in life right now and provides you with much-needed instruction. Read it from page one all the way to the end to get the full benefit. Take time to pause and meditate along the way and ingest its powerful truths into your spirit and mind.

Rick Renner
Minister, Author, Broadcaster
Moscow, Russia

There has been no time in history more exciting than right here, right now. With all the victories we've seen, we must also understand that the enemy is not going away easily. It is imperative that we understand spiritual warfare now more than ever. Joseph Z does a great job blending stories of historic battles from the Bible with current events in *Punishing the Darkness*. Is Artificial Intelligence really an enemy we need to be aware of? Find out inside these pages. We often want the victory, but we don't know how to fight the battle. This book will open your eyes not only to the war before us but also to how to fight it and access the victory we already have in Jesus Christ. Read on and embrace the warrior spirit God has planted inside you!

Gene Bailey
FlashPoint

In this urgent hour of prophetic convergence, Joseph Z has delivered a powerful manual for the modern believer—*Punishing the Darkness* is not just a book; it is a spiritual arsenal forged in the fires of revelation, intercession, and bold Holy Ghost authority. With piercing prophetic clarity and rich biblical insight, Joseph exposes the devil's strategies—from ancient strongholds to end-time deceptions including AI, climate agendas, and technocratic manipulation. He also exposes godly spiritual warfare that works, rooted in the eternal Word and ignited by the fire of the Holy Spirit. As I read these pages, I was stirred in my spirit. Joseph walks readers through the veil, showing not only how to stand against the powers of darkness but how to punish them—tormenting the tormentors through Scripture, prayer, and Spirit-led discernment. Every chapter is a trumpet blast, calling the remnant to rise up, reject passive Christianity, and walk in their Kingdom authority as end-time warriors. This book is for those who sense the shaking and want to know what to do. For intercessors, preachers, watchmen, and prophetic voices—it's time to engage. And Joseph Z has given us the tools to do it with courage, clarity, and conviction.

Perry Stone Jr.
Voice of Evangelism Ministry
www.perrystone.org

I highly endorse Joseph Z's *Punishing the Darkness*. This insightful book explores spiritual warfare, offering practical guidance on renewing the mind and the transformative power of prayer. With clear examples and profound wisdom, Joseph empowers readers to overcome every evil the enemy throws at them, helping them navigate challenges with strength and hope. Enjoy and watch your spiritual growth EXPLODE!

Sid Roth
Host, *It's Supernatural*

In an age of mounting deception and passive Christianity, we must emphasize the identity of the true *Ekklesia*—God's victorious "called-out ones" bringing His Kingdom to earth. In this book, Joseph Z, a good friend and a prophet in our apostolic network, does just that. He presents crucial insights from the Word of God and boldly applies them to issues that are germane to believers everywhere. I believe this is the generation that will see the Church's finest hours, "and the gates of hell shall not prevail against it" (Matthew 16:18).

Dr. Ché Ahn
Senior Leader, Harvest Rock Church, Pasadena, California
President, Harvest International Ministry
International Chancellor, Wagner University

When I first saw the title *Punishing the Darkness*, I was immediately stirred with anticipation. Why? It's time we shift our perspective and strategy in spiritual warfare. In the 1980s and 1990s, trailblazing leaders like Cindy Jacobs, C. Peter Wagner, and George Otis Jr. laid the foundational groundwork in this vital area. With this new book, Joseph Z—writing powerfully as both prophet and teacher—builds on that essential foundation and calls believers to take the "fight" to the enemy's camp. This book isn't just another manual on battling darkness, it's a prophetic blueprint to disciple and deploy believers to tread upon serpents, scorpions, and *all* the power of the enemy. The principles Joseph shares don't merely inform, they activate. You won't finish this book feeling like you're constantly responding to the enemy's attacks, cleaning up the "messes" he makes. Instead, you will step into a place of offensive victory, reclaiming territory and establishing the authority Jesus intended for you to walk in. *Punishing the Darkness* is a timely and vital call to arms for every believer who refuses to live on the defensive and is ready to advance the Kingdom boldly. I cannot recommend it highly enough.

Larry Sparks, MDiv
Publisher, Destiny Image
Author, *Pentecostal Fire*
larrysparksministries.com

Joseph Z's *Punishing the Darkness* is more than a book—it's a battle plan for every believer who refuses to sit idly by while the enemy advances. With prophetic clarity, biblical depth, and practical strategies, Joseph pulls back the veil on the spiritual and cultural warfare of our time. He addresses the real issues facing the Church today—demonic deception, the rise of globalist agendas, and the technological snares that are setting the stage for the last days. This is not a book that merely informs; it equips. You will be challenged to rise up in the authority you have in Christ, to walk in discernment, and to push back against the schemes of the enemy. If you want to be on the front lines—victorious, alert, and effective—this book will show you how. I highly recommend it to every believer who understands that now is the time to stand.

Pastor Todd Coconato
Todd Coconato Ministries
www.PastorTodd.org

I wholeheartedly recommend *Punishing the Darkness* by the prophet Joseph Z—not just as a powerful resource on spiritual warfare but as a reflection of the man who wrote it. Joseph and Heather Z are people of deep integrity, sound doctrine, and supernatural biblical insight. Prophet Z carries a rare blend of revelatory vision and clear, common-sense teaching that equips believers to push back the darkness and release the light of heaven. He doesn't glorify the devil but instead empowers the reader to stand in their God-given authority and take territory for the Kingdom. This book is a vital tool for every believer—and especially for pastors and local churches who want to train up saints to combat hell without veering into the spooky or sensational. *Punishing the Darkness* will help you discern, declare, and demonstrate victory in Christ. Read it, apply it, and watch darkness flee.

Brian Gibson
Pastor, His Church
Gibson Ministries

When I received the manuscript of Joseph Z's new book *Punishing the Darkness,* I immediately felt that even the title itself is prophetic. We are living in a time when the body of Christ is being raised up to do exactly that—to begin punishing the darkness! In the midst of the unprecedented global upheaval and daily turmoil, I've observed many believers retreating from spiritual warfare. But as I read this book, I felt the strength of God rising up in my spirit, stirring a boldness to want to run into battle, not away from it. One of my favorite themes in *Punishing the Darkness* is this: "A man or woman with God outnumbers an army without God." As believers, we really don't have any mountains—our greatest obstacle has often been our ignorance of what God has already done for us in Christ. Joseph Z makes it clear: we are not fighting for victory, but from a position of victory. This book is more than a read—it's a field manual. It's a practical, no-nonsense approach that is immediately applicable to real-life spiritual battles. These are not mere theories; they're proven truths that equip you for the fight. As I read, I could not help but think of the powerful Moravian missionary cry: "May the Lamb who was slain receive the reward of His suffering." Jesus paid the highest price for our redemption, and *Punishing the Darkness* reminds us that His sacrifice demands more than passivity—it calls us to aggressive spiritual warfare. I believe this book will stir the anointing of God in your life, strengthen your resolve, and equip you to confront the powers of darkness head-on.

Mark Cowart
Pastor, Church For All Nations
Colorado Springs, Colorado

Over the years, I have found Joseph Z to be a diligent student of the Bible and an unapologetic preacher and teacher of the irrefutable *Word of God,* known as the Bible! If you are looking for a page-turning powerhouse of a book that will help you experience victory in your daily spiritual battles, read *Punishing the Darkness: Spiritual Warfare That Works* now.

Clay Clark
US SBA Entrepreneur of the Year
ThrivetimeShow.com Podcast Host
Bestselling Author, Recording Artist
Founder, ReAwaken America Tour

In a time of widespread spiritual confusion and turmoil, *Punishing the Darkness* by Joseph Z delivers a bold, clear, and deeply biblical strategy for confronting the forces of evil. This is not just another theological writing, it is a spiritual battle plan for believers committed to walking in the full authority given to us by Jesus Christ. With prophetic insight, historical depth, and a firm grounding in Scripture, Joseph Z unveils the very real war being waged in our world today. From demonic influences shaping civic life to the seductive deception of AI, climate ideologies, and identity distortion, this book fearlessly exposes the enemy's tactics while equipping the Church to rise in truth, power, and prayer. Each chapter offers practical strategies, rich biblical exposition, and a passionate call to action. Whether exploring the spiritual implications of the Tower of Babel or the preservation of Jesus' bloodline, Joseph Z masterfully connects ancient battles to today's spiritual crises with clarity and urgency. This book is for those who are ready to take spiritual warfare seriously—not with fear, but with faith and authority. *Punishing the Darkness* reminds us that we are not victims of our times but victors through Christ. We are called to confront darkness, reclaim lost ground, and advance the Kingdom of God with courage and conviction. Prepare to be equipped, empowered, and emboldened. This is more than a book—it is a spiritual battle plan for those ready to fight.

Dr. Charles Karuku
Lead Pastor, The Hub
Burnsville, Minnesota
TheHubNation.com

There's a reason we don't go home to heaven as soon as we are saved. It's because we have a role to play for the Kingdom of God while we're here on earth. And Joseph Z's new book, *Punishing the Darkness*, will help us all be more aware and effective in the battles we face and the spheres of influence we are called to. I love Joseph's gifting, ministry, and heart for God. But I also deeply appreciate his commitment to the body of Christ. Thank you, Joseph, my friend, for *Punishing the Darkness* and for equipping us all to be more effective and more impactful in our callings and assignments. This book is more than a call to action and more than a training manual. It is an antidote to fear and an amplifier of impact. Darkness doesn't stand a chance!

Robert Hotchkin
Founder, Robert Hotchkin Ministries
and Men on the Frontlines
roberthotchkin.com

This book is a timely read that gives powerful language and strategy for the hour we're living in. It's a weapon in the hands of every believer—equipping us to walk in our God-given authority, swing the sword of the Spirit, and torment every spirit of darkness! A true field manual for those ready to take their place on the frontlines!

Matt Cruz
Evangelist
MattCruz.com

What an incredible book! Get ready to be activated! Once again, Joseph has given a powerful gift to the body of Christ. *Punishing the Darkness* is packed with tremendous insight to help believers navigate the end times, current events, and the questions so many are asking, but few are answering with a true biblical perspective. With his prophetic gift and solid biblical foundation, Joseph offers more than just revelation—he provides practical application for what we're called to do right now. While many voices focus on how dark the world has become, Joseph grounds us in Scripture and floods the reader with real hope. There's a reason he's known as the "Grace Prophet"—not another doom-and-gloom voice pointing out the obvious, but a true prophetic guide equipping the Church. In this book, he dives into the battle of the mind, different types of prayer, and spiritual warfare, and exposes the enemy's tactics with clarity and wisdom. Reading this book will not only fill you with revelation—it will activate you to *Punish the Darkness!*

Ben Diaz
Author, *Radical Healing*
Senior Pastor, Vida Church, Mesa, Arizona
radicalhealingbook.com; vidachurchaz.com; IG@pastorbendiaz

One of the things I love about Joseph Z's ministry, his teaching, and this book is his God-given ability to help you see things from a new perspective and a victorious mindset. As you read *Punishing the Darkness,* you will see current events in a new light. However, you will not be terrified by the news reports. You will be emboldened and armed to make a difference. Spiritual warfare is real. However, many have fictitious beliefs about it. In this book, Joseph helps you adopt a biblical mindset concerning this popular topic and provides practical ways for you to implement what you learn. The finest hour of the Church has arrived. The attacks of darkness will not stop us. *Punishing the Darkness: Spiritual Warfare That Works* will help you live a victorious life and overcome all the attacks of the wicked one.

Kerrick Butler
Pastor, Faith Christian Center
Mableton, Georgia

Punishing the Darkness is a major answer for the whole body of Christ to learn how to effectively enforce the devil's defeat! The amount of knowledge, revelation, and understanding about the devil and his tactics causes every one of us to stand firm in faith, knowing Jesus has conquered him on our behalf. This book teaches a present-day truth about the real warfare we're in, and how we are assured we can win! It exposes details of Satan's hidden agenda using various modern entities, some cultural mindsets, and more details of how much we've allowed demonic forces to infiltrate just about every area of society. It truly explains today's spiritual warfare in detail. Learning the principles set forth in *Punishing the Darkness* provides the necessary revelation to see and know ahead of time how to pray prophetically against enemy onslaughts to steal, kill, and destroy. It teaches how to unlock things not seen in the hidden spiritual realm, so we can be prepared to deal with them to defeat the devil's agenda. Joseph Z has laid out a battle plan with divine instructions that anyone can follow by teaching us who we are, what we are called to do, and how we can accomplish it by gaining truth about the devil. In this book, he teaches us spiritual weapons that are in our hands to cause us to stand strong to help birth this awesome move of God! I highly recommend this book to everyone who intends to live a life of freedom and victory!

Ginger Ziegler
Gingerziegler.com
Pastor, Teacher, Author

I wholeheartedly recommend Joseph Z's book, *Punishing the Darkness.* As a long-time friend, I've witnessed his deep commitment to faith, and this book is a powerful testament to that. Joseph explores the critical subjects of spiritual warfare and the need to overcome the evil we face in our world today. He expertly emphasizes the importance of making the Word of God central in our lives. This book will inspire and equip you to stand firm in your faith and navigate life's challenges with strength and purpose. Don't miss the opportunity to experience the transformative insights Joseph shares within these pages!

Joshua Ercoli
Founder, Souled Out International

Many books on the market today explore the topic of spiritual warfare, examining its relevance in our turbulent world. But Joseph Z's new book offers so much more! *Punishing the Darkness: Spiritual Warfare That Works* cuts through the noise and delivers practical, no-nonsense tools to help you secure victory and punish the darkness in every arena of your life. We've all heard the adage, "A mind is a terrible thing to waste." It's more than a catchy phrase—it's a profound truth. Our lives are the direct result of the thoughts that fill our minds. While Joseph addresses multiple key principles for winning spiritual battles, he emphasizes that the mind is the central battlefield. The devil can only devour what we surrender! If we're "sober-minded" and rooted in the Word of God, the enemy will roar like a lion, seeking to shake our foundation and gain access to our thoughts. But when we renew our minds with the Word of God, by faith, take every thought captive, and stand in our God-given authority, we slam that door in the devil's face. Joseph carefully outlines the covenant truths of our identity and authority in Jesus Christ and shifts the narrative with his powerful declaration, "Going Red"—a reference to the life-changing power of the blood of Jesus. Through that finished work of the cross and our full surrender to Jesus, Joseph reminds us that no power in hell can stand against the Greater One who lives in us. We aren't just called to push back against evil, we are empowered to punish the darkness.

Kyle Loffelmacher
Publisher
Harrison House

Punishing the Darkness is a bold, Spirit-empowered guide to spiritual warfare that actually works. Joseph Z equips believers to move from survival mode to supernatural offense—breaking strongholds, silencing demonic attacks, and reclaiming ground the enemy has stolen. This isn't theory—it's strategy forged in fire. If you're ready to torment your spiritual tormentors, this book will show you how.

Shaun Tabatt
Author, *The NDE Conspiracy*

PUNISHING THE DARKNESS

Harrison House Books by Joseph Z

Punishing the Darkness: Spiritual Warfare That Works

Demystifying the Prophetic: Understanding the Voice of God for the Coming Days of Fire

The Secret to the Life of John: A Revelation for a Supernaturally Long-Lasting Life

Servants of Fire: Secrets of the Unseen War & Angels Fighting for You

Breaking Hell's Economy: Your Guide to Last-Days Supernatural Provision

Breaking Hell's Economy Study Manual

The Spirit of Elijah: Expose the Truth. Embrace God's Power. Break the Antichrist Spirit.

The Spirit of Elijah Study Manual

A Prophet's Reward: Partnering with the Prophetic for Your Faith, Favor, and Financial Miracles

Weaponizing Your Faith: Supernaturally Equipped to Receive Your Breakthrough

The Origin of the Cosmic Battle

Jesus and the Kingmakers

PUNISHING THE DARKNESS

SPIRITUAL WARFARE THAT WORKS

JOSEPH Z

© Copyright 2026– Joseph Z

Printed in the United States of America. All rights reserved. No portion of this book may be reproduced, stored in a retrieval system, or transmitted in any form or by any means—electronic, mechanical, photocopy, recording, scanning, or other—except for brief quotations in critical reviews or articles, without the prior written permission of the publisher.

Unless otherwise identified, Scripture quotations are taken from the New King James Version. Copyright © 1982 by Thomas Nelson, Inc. Used by permission. All rights reserved.

Scripture quotations marked KJV are taken from the King James Version.

Scripture quotations marked NIV are taken from the HOLY BIBLE, NEW INTERNATIONAL VERSION®, Copyright © 1973, 1978, 1984, 2011 International Bible Society. Used by permission of Zondervan. All rights reserved.

Scripture quotations marked NLT are taken from the Holy Bible, New Living Translation, copyright 1996, 2004, 2015. Used by permission of Tyndale House Publishers., Wheaton, Illinois 60189. All rights reserved.

Scripture quotations marked AMP are taken from the Amplified® Bible, Copyright © 2015 by The Lockman Foundation, La Habra, CA 90631. All rights reserved. Used by permission.

Scripture quotations marked AMPC are taken from the Amplified® Bible, Classic Edition, Copyright © 1954, 1958, 1962, 1964, 1965, 1987 by The Lockman Foundation. All rights reserved. Used by permission.

Scripture quotations marked NASB are taken from the NEW AMERICAN STANDARD BIBLE®, Copyright © 1960, 1962, 1963, 1968, 1971, 1972, 1973, 1975, 1977, 1995, 2020 by The Lockman Foundation. Used by permission.

All emphasis within Scripture quotations is the author's own.

Published by Harrison House Publishers
Shippensburg, PA 17257

ISBN 13 TP: 978-1-6675-1197-9
ISBN 13 eBook: 978-1-6675-1198-6

For Worldwide Distribution, Printed in the U.S.A.
2 3 4 5 6 7 8 / 30 29 28 27 26

DEDICATION

Spiritual warfare is majorly pushed to a place of victory by those who know how to fellowship with God, mingle the Word of God with their faith, and be led by the Holy Spirit while praying fervently. Of all God's people who pray, I would like to specifically dedicate this book to praying grandmothers. We know that all believers are called to pray. Yet in my experience, when grandmothers pray, there is a special voltage released against darkness. My grandmother was a force in prayer that changed my life, and that same dedicated intercession has been carried on by my mother and now my wife.

To each grandmother who goes to war on behalf of your children and children's children, you are crucial to the plan of God for the future of our generations—this is for you.

I honor you and want to express how much God sees you and what a deep level of thanks the body of Christ owes you. Many times, you are unseen, but you are fierce in the spirit and are a destructive agent against the powers of darkness. Praying grandmas have played a crucial role through prayer that has seen wars won, lives saved, the sick healed, and most importantly, the lost coming home to Jesus. You are heroes, and it was on my heart to dedicate this book to you. Thank God for you.

Sincerely,
Joseph Z

ACKNOWLEDGMENTS

First and always, my amazing wife, Heather, followed by our children and now grandbaby! You are my best friends. Thank you for your constant support while I wrote this book and the many projects like it that you assist me with every day. I love each one of you.

Without each of the tremendous people I am surrounded by every day, the message of such a book as this one would not find its highest destination. To my staff and team, each of you is world-class, and it is a privilege to work with you to impact the world for Jesus.

To my editors, Mary Ercoli and Barb Wiles, thank you for the tremendous work you dedicated to this book and for your unwavering support of all our written projects.

CONTENTS

FOREWORD BY MIKE SIGNORELLI

Most Christians today are losing spiritual battles they don't even realize they're fighting. After years in deliverance ministry, praying for thousands trapped in cycles that medical intervention alone couldn't break, I've witnessed how spiritual battles require spiritual weapons. I've seen people instantly freed when we moved from merely resisting darkness to actively enforcing Christ's victory through focused, Scripture-based warfare.

When Joseph Z asked me to write the foreword for *Punishing the Darkness*, I recognized immediately that this book addresses the core issue: most believers don't understand the authority they carry. They're fighting spiritual battles with natural solutions, wondering why they keep losing ground to an enemy Jesus already defeated.

Joseph understands this reality in profound ways. What sets his approach apart is how he connects ancient biblical truths with the spiritual battles we face today. His examination of Elisha's encounter in 2 Kings 6 reveals something powerful: Elisha didn't just defeat his enemies; he left them confused and wandering away defeated. That's the kind of comprehensive victory God intends for us.

Having been raised in poverty and dysfunction, I've spent years researching how trauma and behavior patterns pass through generations. Modern science now reinforces biblical principles about renewing our minds, and Joseph's treatment of the mind as the primary battlefield particularly resonates with me. He masterfully brings these concepts together without getting lost in either extreme psychology or mystical thinking.

The distinction Joseph makes between defensive and offensive spiritual warfare addresses a significant gap in modern Christian teaching. Too many believers only know how to "resist the devil" without understanding they have the authority to go on the attack. Joseph's concept of "punishing" dark powers isn't about revenge; it's about enforcing the victory Jesus already secured.

What makes this book particularly valuable is Joseph's systematic approach to spiritual engagement. Rather than offering feel-good platitudes, he provides practical, Scripture-based strategies that work. His warfare prayers aren't devotional exercises; they're battle-tested tools for believers who understand their authority in Christ. The book's structure moves logically from foundational principles through specific applications, covering everything from generational curses to contemporary cultural deceptions.

Throughout this work, Joseph maintains a crucial balance. He recognizes real spiritual conflict without falling into paranoia or superstition. He acknowledges genuine spiritual opposition while affirming the decisive victory of Christ. This balance is essential for believers who must navigate both the reality of spiritual warfare and the confidence that comes from understanding their position in Christ.

This book arrives at a critical time in church history. As Western Christianity increasingly faces ideological and spiritual challenges, believers need more than motivational encouragement. They need a solid biblical framework for understanding and engaging these battles. Joseph provides exactly that: a biblically sound, practically applicable approach to spiritual warfare that moves beyond individual victory toward cultural transformation.

The principles outlined here speak to the Church's role in generational change and the practical outworking of kingdom authority in today's world. This work will transform you from someone who merely survives spiritual battles to someone who enforces heaven's victory on earth.

I recommend this book to pastors, ministry leaders, and believers who recognize that our current cultural moment requires both spiritual discernment and practical wisdom. Joseph Z has provided both in remarkable measure.

Mike Signorelli
Lead Pastor of V1 Church
Author of *Inherit Your Freedom: Break Free from Generational Curses*

FOREWORD BY ALAN DIDIO

More Americans believe in aliens and UFOs than believe in God. That fact alone should be enough to wake us up. We are watching our nation teeter on the edge of being overtaken by end-time deception, but I believe there's still hope. I believe God is raising up a remnant to stand against this Noah-like flood of darkness, and that's why this book is so important.

Punishing the Darkness is a prophetic strike against that flood. Joseph Z doesn't simply describe the war we're in; he shows us how to win it. His bold declaration is that we are not helpless victims… we are authorized warriors. And now more than ever, we must rise and take our place.

> *Be sober, be vigilant; because your adversary the devil, as a roaring lion, walketh about, seeking whom he may devour* (1 Peter 5:8 KJV).

I know you've felt the weight of this warfare. The enemy has assaulted your health, attacked your family, and undermined your confidence in God. He's used people, problems, distractions, and discouragements to wear you down. But hear me clearly, his days are numbered in your life. Your warfare is shifting!

Watchman Nee, a Chinese church leader and author known for his powerful teachings on spiritual authority and victorious Christian living, once observed that one of the greatest weaknesses a believer can have is not hating the devil enough. We've allowed the enemy far too much ground. We've tolerated his interference, accepted his harassment, and explained away his attacks as just another part of life. But no more.

We must stop excusing the devil's presence and start confronting it. We should not shrug and say, "Oh well, it's just another attack." No, if we want to operate in a new dimension of spiritual authority, we must mark every violation, every trespass, every assault, and bring it before the Righteous Judge. There is no comparison between the power of our adversary and the power of our God, but even the most powerful judge cannot rule on a case that hasn't been presented.

Jesus taught this in the parable of the persistent widow who cried out, "Avenge me of mine adversary." The enemy had violated her territory, and she wasn't about to let it go unchallenged. What a picture of the Church in this hour! We've been assaulted, slandered, and stolen from, but now, it's time to go before the throne and demand justice.

This end-time prayer, combined with the revelation in this book, will *Punish the Darkness.* We're not commanded to avoid seeking vengeance; we're instructed not to take it into our own hands. Instead, we are called to seek it from Heaven. If we don't, justice can be delayed. But when we persist, vengeance is promised.

How have you been attacked this week? How has the enemy dared to touch what belongs to you? It's outrageous that satan would lay a hand on a child of God, but even more outrageous is when that child says nothing in response. When was the last time you stood in prayer and pleaded for justice? When was the last time you brought a formal accusation before the Judge of Heaven?

This is one of the core truths of the parable in Luke 18: Don't stop seeking justice from Heaven against your adversary! God has chosen not to act alone. He has chosen to act through us. That's not just a responsibility, it's a privilege. We get to partner with Him in enforcing the victory of the Cross over Satan.

That's where *Punishing the Darkness* comes in. In this book, Joseph Z exposes the reason so many believers feel under constant spiritual attack... because they are! But rather than settle for merely surviving the demonic pressure or praying powerless prayers, Brother Z equips you to strike back with precision. Your warfare is about to shift. The tables are turning, and in this book, you'll learn how to become a torment to your spiritual tormentors.

> *The God of peace shall bruise Satan under your feet shortly. The grace of our Lord Jesus Christ be with you. Amen* (Romans 16:20 KJV).

Alan DiDio
Pastor of The Encounter Charlotte
Host of *Encounter Today*

SECTION 1

CONFRONTING THE SPIRIT OF THE AGE

CHAPTER ONE

PUNISHING DARK POWERS

And Elisha prayed, and said, "LORD, I pray, open his eyes that he may see." Then the LORD opened the eyes of the young man, and he saw. And behold, the mountain was full of horses and chariots of fire all around Elisha.

—2 Kings 6:17

As the early morning sun broke over the horizon, onlookers from the small city of Dothan were met with a shocking sight. Unlike previous mornings, which offered peaceful views in every direction with avenues for locals and travelers to come and go, today, every vantage point was blocked by the startling sight of mighty horses, chariots of war, and a great wall of armed soldiers standing at attention.

Dothan was a small city by today's standards, at 25 acres in size, which must have added to the already growing anxiety every local might have been experiencing from this unsettling picture. There was no path of escape, as this military presence encompassed and surrounded the entirety of the city perimeter. Under orders from the king of Syria, this army had been marshaled to encompass the whole city. For what purpose? To identify and capture a supernatural codebreaker, the one who had been divulging the plans and strategies of Syria's king. The army had come to apprehend God's man, who revealed the enemy's plans and secrets in advance—Elisha was in the city, and the king was retaliating.

THE SERVANT'S VANTAGE POINT

Therefore he sent horses and chariots and a great army there, and they came by night and surrounded the city. [15] *And when the servant of the man of God arose early and went out, there was an army, surrounding the city with horses and chariots. And his servant said to him, "Alas, my master! What shall we do?"* [16] *So he answered, "Do not fear, for those who are with us are more than those who are with them."*

—2 Kings 6:14-16

That morning, Elisha's servant arose early and witnessed this massive gathering of armed men and their horses and chariots. Fear struck him as he said, "Alas, my master! What shall we do?" Elisha confidently answered his servant, "Do not fear, for those who are with us are more than those who are with them."What a statement! Seeing how outnumbered they were, the man of God commented,"Do not fear, we are not outnumbered, we are the majority today."

From this moment, Elisha doesn't just make a statement—as we see in 2 Kings 6:17: "Elisha prayed, and said, 'Lord, I pray, open his eyes that he may see.'Then the Lord opened the eyes of the young man, and he saw. And behold, the mountain was full of horses and chariots of fire all around Elisha."

Imagine the look on the servant's face when he had his spiritual eyes opened and the boldness that must have come over him in this moment! Elisha's servant might have gone from "Oh no, what are we going to do?" To, "Hey, you little boys up there! What are you going to do? Come and get us!" While laughing and pointing. What happened next is a remarkable example of God's intervention.

So when the Syrians came down to him, Elisha prayed to the LORD, and said, "Strike this people, I pray, with blindness." And He struck them with blindness according to the word of Elisha.

—2 Kings 6:18

In 2 Kings 6:18, the Syrians must have identified Elisha and his servant because they started approaching them from an elevated position around the city. At this moment, as the army was marching toward them, the prophet and his servant were not looking at the forces of man; they were now looking at the forces of heaven. Faith must have been on Elisha as that military force moved to apprehend the prophet. At this moment, Elisha opened his mouth and prayed to the Lord, saying, "Strike this people, I pray, with blindness." The Lord struck them with blindness according to the word of Elisha!

A MAN WITH GOD OUTNUMBERS AN ARMY WITHOUT GOD

Following this prayer, a shift of power occurred. Blindness struck the entire Syrian army. In one moment, all their military might and strength fell into the hands of one old man who happened to have God on his side.

> *Now Elisha said to them, "This is not the way, nor is this the city. Follow me, and I will bring you to the man whom you seek." But he led them to Samaria.*
>
> —2 Kings 6:19

Amazingly, what happened next was that Elisha led them through the wilderness. Imagine the sight of that! An old man walking out in front of the entire army, leading them. God must have a sense of humor. After all, He is the one who sits in the heavens and laughs at the plans of man and all their might (*see* Psalm 2:4).

TEN MILES LEADING A BLIND ARMY

> *So it was, when they had come to Samaria, that Elisha said, "LORD, open the eyes of these men, that they may see." And the LORD opened their eyes, and they saw; and there they were, inside Samaria!* 21 *Now when the king of Israel saw them, he said to Elisha, "My father, shall I kill them? Shall I kill them?"*
>
> —2 Kings 6:20-21

Elisha led these men ten miles through the wilderness into the region of Samaria.[1] When the king of Israel saw what was happening, he was delighted at such a great chance of vengeance that he said to Elisha, "My father, shall I kill them? Shall I kill them?" Elisha led the Syrians in their blindness straight into the city of Samaria, where they suddenly found themselves at the mercy of the king and his troops. Elisha responded to the king of Israel, saying:

> *But he answered, "You shall not kill them. Would you kill those whom you have taken captive with your sword and your bow? Set food and water before them, that they may eat and drink and go to their master."* 23 *Then he prepared a great feast for them; and after they ate and drank, he sent them away and they went to their master. So the bands of Syrian raiders came no more into the land of Israel.*
>
> —2 Kings 6:22-23

Elisha graciously allowed the army to leave unharmed. I'm sure they would not have attempted to retaliate at that moment because they feared the blindness could be reinstated, and they would have been slaughtered with ease.

GOD WILL SURROUND YOUR ENEMIES

> *Now to Him who is able to do exceedingly abundantly above all that we ask or think, according to the power that works in us.*
>
> —Ephesians 3:20

God, who can do exceedingly and abundantly more than we can ask or think, granted Elisha the favor and power to transform his situation. Instead of being surrounded, he found himself in a position where those surrounding him were now encircled by their mortal enemies.[2]

> ***"The Christian on his knees can see more than the philosopher on his tiptoes."***
>
> —Saint Augustine of Hippo

GOD IS GREATER!

When considering this narrative with Elisha and the Syrian army, we must take into account what the apostle John stated in 1 John 4:4, when he wrote,

"You are of God, little children, and have overcome them, because He who is in you is greater than he who is in the world."

That is the revelation Jesus gave us. Greater is He, Jesus, than he, the spirit of Antichrist in the world. As believers, our fight is to discern the greater reality, which is a daily fight in our lives; yet, much like Elisha, who told his servant, *there are far more on our side than there are right here in the natural battle we are facing.* How do we engage the Spirit of the Living God and take action against the wicked forces of darkness? As you will discover, there are levels to victory that God has given us, and it is your responsibility, dear reader, to uncover and activate what is available to you in your life.

EXECUTING VENGEANCE ON THE DARKNESS

> *Let the saints be joyful in glory; let them sing aloud on their beds.* [6] *Let the high praises of God be in their mouth, and a two-edged sword in their hand,* [7] *to execute vengeance on the nations, and punishments on the peoples;* [8] *to bind their kings with chains, and their nobles with fetters of iron;* [9] *to execute on them the written judgment—this honor have all His saints. Praise the LORD!*
>
> —Psalm 149:5-9

When we stand up as believers, we must know we have rights in the spirit realm. Psalm 149:6 says it well: "Let the high praises of God be in their mouth, and a two-edged sword in their hand."

Here we see two things:

1. **High praise in the mouth** of the believer. Praise is an act of war against the powers of darkness.
2. **A two-edged sword in their hand.** This represents the Word of God active in the life of the believer.

Next, we see in Psalm 149:7 the purpose of those two acts of war. Praise and the Word of God activate the authority to take specific actions when in proper use. Here, they are to *execute vengeance on the nations.* For the New Testament believer, this is not a physical act of war because the Old Testament is written for our benefit and offers spiritual insights into how we are to contend today. This means we can take spiritual vengeance on dark powers behind nations, such as demonic forces and rulers in high places.

Additionally, verse 7 continues by saying, "...and punishments on the peoples...." Again, a point of reference to the forces of evil—driving people who do evil, such as terrorism, or acts against society that violate the Word of God. Verse 8 continues, saying, "...to *bind their kings with chains* and their *nobles with fetters of iron....*" This is the act of binding and loosing the powers behind those in authority, whether they are the head of a nation, organization, or those under them with lower authority.

Verse 9 ties it together: "To *execute on them the written judgment*—This honor have all His saints." "Written judgment" means believers use the Word of God to pray and authorize what is written. Use your free moral agency in prayer and cooperation with the Scripture. Finally, we see that it is our honor as saints of God to do so! That's right; it is your honor, dear reader, as a believer in Jesus Christ and your standing as a saint to enforce these spiritual actions through prayer.

Punishing darkness goes beyond simply rebuking a demon or an evil force. It means you give direction by wielding the Word of God in worship and releasing the written Word of God over any situation with your faith.

ELISHA DID MORE THAN SEND THE ENEMIES AWAY, HE SHOWED THEM COMPLETE DEFEAT

Elisha didn't just overcome the enemies he faced, nor did he run them off. Instead, he captured them and took them to a position where their enemies surrounded them! This was a form of sowing and reaping for evil. It is also powerful to recognize that God will position His people to release spiritual torment onto the spiritual tormentors. Binding spiritual forces is powerful, but punishing them means leaving them disheartened and wandering away to the point they fear coming back at you.

> *Having disarmed principalities and powers, He made a public spectacle of them, triumphing over them in it.*
>
> —Colossians 2:15

Jesus did this when He made an open display of the powers of darkness in Colossians 2:15.

God defends His own, especially when they cooperate with Him and use the authority He gave them to walk in. When thinking about the story of Elisha and how he stood up to the forces of evil, many scriptures come to mind:

> *The angel of the LORD encampeth round them that fear Him, and delivereth them.*
>
> —Psalm 34:7 KJV

> *For he shall give his angels charge over thee, to keep thee in all thy ways.*
>
> —Psalm 91:11 KJV

> *And I will encamp about mine house because of the army, because of him that passeth by, and because of him that returneth: and no oppressor shall pass through them any more: for now have I seen with mine eyes.*
>
> —Zechariah 9:8 KJV

> *In all their affliction He was afflicted, and the Angel of His Presence saved them: in His love and in His pity He redeemed them; and He bare them and carried them all the days of old.*
>
> —Isaiah 63:9

TIME TO TORMENT YOUR SPIRITUAL TORMENTORS

> *Casting down arguments and every high thing that exalts itself against the knowledge of God, bringing every thought into captivity to the obedience of Christ,* [6] *and being ready to* ***punish all disobedience*** *when your obedience is fulfilled.*
>
> —2 Corinthians 10:5-6

Ultimately, if we are going to punish the darkness, it comes through understanding, and understanding, when put to practice by faith, turns into revelation. Revelation, by definition, is *revealed knowledge to your spirit man.* From the position of praying the Word out loud regarding any issue or topic, especially when marshaled toward spiritual forces of evil, there will come a revelatory release of punishment on darkness.

Second Corinthians 10:6 says we are to punish our disobedience first. Punishment of evil comes from a position of authority, which is a by-product of obeying God and the Word. Warfare is won at the highest level when the believer takes control of their thoughts and obeys God. From this position, there is authority to release the Word of God in faith against the adversary. A truly submitted person to the Word and will of God Almighty becomes a force of torment to our adversaries. You, dear reader, are called to be a punishing force and a torment to your spiritual tormentors. Keep reading your Bible, mix it with your faith, stand firm on the promises, obey God, and it will bring great torment to whatever is tormenting you!

CHAPTER TWO

THE SECOND DARK TOWER

The fifth angel sounded his trumpet, and I saw a star that had fallen from the sky to the earth. The star was given the key to the shaft of the Abyss.[2] ***When he opened the Abyss, smoke rose from it like the smoke from a gigantic furnace.*** *The sun and sky were darkened by the smoke from the Abyss.*

—Revelation 9:1-2 NIV

In this chapter, I would like you to consider what dark powers might be plotting for the future and how much evil we, the *Ekklesia* (the Church), are restraining. We will compare two dark towers of humanity, one ancient and the other modern. Each was built to reach out to the realm of the unseen without God's authorization. The purpose of comparing these is to show where society will always navigate without intervention.

Ultimately, these wicked plans will come to their full, deceptive destination and complete cooperation with evil forces from the spirit realm. It must be understood that from the fall of rebellious angels in Genesis 6, all the way to the opening of the abyss in Revelation 9, the endgame for darkness is the same—free rein on humanity by the permission of society itself.

CERN AND THE TOWER OF BABEL

The two dark towers I will compare are the ancient Tower of Babel and modern-day CERN. We will look at interesting parallels between the two—

ultimately, the point I want to make is that they are driven by the same spirit. We will begin by observing the Tower of Babel.

SPIRITUAL FORCES OPERATE BY PERMISSION FOR ACCESS

Spiritual forces cannot *invade* humanity without cooperation from humankind. A powerful truth is the realization that Jesus was not on earth in the Old Testament narrative, but today, because of Jesus' life, death, and resurrection, we have an atmosphere reset for us to work in. As the *Ekklesia*, the Church of the Lord Jesus Christ, we stand as a restraining force to all the wickedness that eagerly desires its day.

Citizens of the ancient world were far more susceptible to the evil schemes of fallen angels, having no mediator, no Savior, no Jesus. Today, we operate within a vastly different scope of authority. Nonetheless, evil wants to rise, and even with Jesus and the Church on earth, deception is propagated by nefarious powers, and sadly, has an audience willing to listen like sheep puppets that will cooperate with these vile forces, giving them as much access into our natural world as they can acquire. Both comparisons we are about to look at ultimately lead toward the opening of the abyss.

Opening the abyss spoken of in Revelation 9 will be far more evil than any human can imagine, and it is possible that humanity will be responsible for it, even if inadvertently, through rogue science experimentation that attempts to tamper with, or even breach, the veil between our natural realm and the unseen.

THE ORIGINAL DARK TOWER

> *Now the whole earth had one language and one speech. [2] And it came to pass, as they journeyed from the east, that they found a plain in the land of Shinar, and they dwelt there. [3] Then they said to one another, "Come, let us make bricks and bake them thoroughly." They had brick for stone, and they had asphalt for mortar. [4] And they said, "Come, let us build ourselves a city, and a tower whose top is in the heavens; let us make a name for ourselves, lest we be scattered abroad over the face of the whole earth." [5] But the LORD came down to see the city and the tower which the sons of men had built. [6] And the LORD said,*

> *"Indeed the people are one and they all have one language, and this is what they begin to do; now nothing that they propose to do will be withheld from them."*
>
> —Genesis 11:1-6

> *Cush begot Nimrod; he began to be a mighty one on the earth.* [9] *He was a mighty hunter before the LORD; therefore it is said, "Like Nimrod the mighty hunter before the LORD."* [10] *And the beginning of his kingdom was Babel, Erech, Accad, and Calneh, in the land of Shinar.*
>
> —Genesis 10:8-10

Babel, with its evil leader, Nimrod, was both a prototype system of the beast and the first version of the man of sin—the Antichrist. What they were constructing in Genesis 11 in that valley of Shinar was likely a massively high ziggurat. Not only was it built to reach remarkable heights, but its operational design was something far more sinister.

LUCIFER HAD HIGH AMBITION

Going high above the clouds was an aspiration of the main fallen angel, Lucifer, who said, "I will ascend above the heights of the clouds; I will be like the most High" (*see* Isaiah 14:14 KJV).

We can only speculate on all the possibilities the Tower of Babel was meddling with. From a place of conjecture, many believe that the Tower of Babel was likely a place of access, opening the realm of the spirit to the natural, acting like a portal, and ultimately allowing any evil beings entrance to our natural domain, with humanity being used to permit them.

WEAPONIZED PAWNS

Nimrod and his followers from the valley of Shinar were likely weaponized pawns attempting to give the earth over to the evil forces behind the veil. What these ancient people were setting out to accomplish through what some speculate was occult worship and alleged mad science was the eventual opening of the bottomless pit in Revelation 9:11. Forbidden knowledge was given to Nimrod and his followers by these watchers—also known as the sons of God, or angels who came down to cohabitate with women in Genesis 6.

If the people of Shinar had opened a spiritual gateway to usher in vile dark forces, it would have rendered the ancient world defenseless to the reign of those watchers and their offspring. Evil beings would rule humanity, let out of the spirit realm, and operate in the natural world. These vile forces would have had full rein of the earth because humanity, like Adam before them, would be the ones who gave their entire world over to complete and final darkness. Had God not intervened, all humanity would have suffered from the open portal at the first dark tower.

Consider Nimrod, their leader, who became a mighty man. Some suggest Nimrod became a mighty man because he was potentially a Nephilim and the original version of the Antichrist. This conclusion is based on the Hebrew word *gib·bōr*, which means *mighty men* or *giants*. We see this same Hebrew word in Genesis 6:4, which says, "There were giants on the earth in those days, and also afterward, when the sons of God came in to the daughters of men and they bore children to them. Those were the *mighty men* who were of old, men of renown."

Nimrod is what I call the anti-Adam, the devil's first attempt at bringing about the man of sin, well before his time.

THE ANTI-ADAM

He was a mighty hunter before the LORD; therefore it is said, "Like Nimrod the mighty hunter before the LORD."

—Genesis 10:9

[Nimrod] said he would be revenged on God, if he should have a mind to drown the world again; for that he would build a tower too high for the waters to reach. And that he would avenge himself on God for destroying their forefathers.

—Antiquities of the Jews, Book 1, Chapter 4

Nimrod, whose name means *we rebel,* ruled Babylon and was the instigator of the famous Tower of Babel, as described in Genesis 11. As I previously stated, Nimrod was the first representation of the Antichrist, and he became a mighty hunter. According to extra-biblical texts, Nimrod was involved in the building of the Tower of Babel. In a sense, Nimrod was attempting to replace Adam, the original son of God. Some consider Nimrod to be the first world ruler, a perversion of what Adam was assigned to do.

Nimrod was responsible for leading the construction of the Tower of Babel. According to Josephus, the motivation for creating the Tower of Babel was to protect humanity from another flood. Further, according to Josephus, Nimrod "persuaded [his subjects] not to ascribe [their strength] to God, as if it were through his means they were happy, but to believe that it was their courage which procured that happiness."[1]

If what Josephus suggested about Nimrod was true, then Nimrod could be classified as a godless, humanistic anti-Adam. Adam, the original son of God who was to rule the garden and subdue the earth, was also referred to in the Bible as the first man, or Adam. Jesus is the last Adam (*see* 1 Corinthians 15:45).

By referring to Nimrod as the anti-Adam, I am saying he carried the original spirit of Antichrist and raised himself to pervert the purpose of God on the earth through rebellion. Rebellion against God is one of the primary purposes of the Antichrist.[2]

Ever since the fall of man, there have been many false religions and ungodly belief systems that attempt to usurp the God of heaven and do things as they wish rather than serve and surrender to the Creator. Much of this is due to the nefarious activities of those mutinous fallen angels who acted according to their will rather than in alignment with God's will. That same spirit has flooded the earth, and we face it today—the spirit of Antichrist. Could we be witnessing this again today through demonic rebellion, under the guise of scientific research? The answer is yes.

THE SECOND DARK TOWER

Let's take a modern-day look at what is a terrible and shocking comparison to the ancient Tower of Babel. A second dark tower has been in operation for many years and may either be the actual means by which we see the abyss opened or a prototype for a future technological marvel that will do so.

CERN AND THE LARGE HADRON COLLIDER

Near Geneva, Switzerland, on the border with France, there is a facility named CERN that spans both the French and Swiss sides of the border. CERN is an acronym for the European Organization for Nuclear Research, and it operates the largest particle physics laboratory in the world, where the renowned Large Hadron Collider, or the LHC, is located. The LHC, called CERN, is the world's largest and most powerful particle accelerator and the largest machine man has ever constructed. CERN is a large underground circle 17 miles long and buried 574 feet beneath the Earth's surface.

In simple terms, the LHC was designed to smash subatomic particles together at or near the speed of light to discover the original particle that initiated the universe a fraction of a second after the "Big Bang," the so-called "God Particle."

Due to its abilities, many eminent physicists believe that the LHC has the potential to destroy not only the world but also the universe itself.

STEPHEN HAWKING'S WARNING

For example, famed English theoretical physicist and cosmologist Stephen Hawking toured the LHC facilities in 2006. He discussed the potential discoveries the new experiments could make, including superpartners, black holes, and the Higgs boson (also known as the God particle). Hawking also expressed startling concerns about the Higgs boson, suggesting that it could potentially lead to a catastrophic vacuum decay, which could wipe out the universe. However, he acknowledged that such an event is unlikely to happen in the near future, given the current economic climate and the scale of the particle accelerator required to trigger such an event.[3]

OPENING A PORTAL

> ***"Out of this door might come something, or we might send something through it...."***
>
> —Sergio Bertolucci, Director for Research and Scientific Computing at CERN

The director of CERN from 2009 to 2015, Sergio Bertolucci, made a troubling statement about the Large Hadron Collider, saying that "it could open a doorway to another dimension, and out this door might come something, or we might send something through it."[4] When observing Bertolucci's statement, it is clear that the researchers and scientists at CERN believe in the existence of outside parallel and even alternative dimensions (physics dictates that there are at least eleven).[5] This suggests that scientists are allegedly attempting to tear open the veil that separates the two by recreating the conditions of the Big Bang.

Notably, the term abyss, or "bottomless pit," is translated from the Greek word, which means "shaft of the abyss." In this context, the abyss is an extremely deep place. It occurs only twice outside the Book of Revelation (Romans 10:7, simply the abode of the dead; Luke 8:31, the prison destined for evil spirits). In Revelation 9:1-2, Revelation 11:7, Revelation 17:8, Revelation 20:1, and Revelation 20:3, it is a prison in which evil powers are confined and out of which they can sometimes be let loose. It is not the lake of fire (Revelation 20:10); nor is Satan regarded as being cast into this prison forever, but only to be so cast for one thousand years (Revelation 20:1-2).[6]

The bottomless pit is implied to be a tunnel leading to the abyss. The concept of a tunnel could be what we understand as a (wormhole),[7] leading to another dimension or a black hole.[8] Interestingly, scientists often use the term "bottomless pit" to refer to a black hole!

In Roman times, where a temple existed in honor of Apollyon the destroyer, the Romans believed this site was a gateway to the underworld, which is significant given the association of the "bottomless pit" with the underworld. Compare this to Revelation 9:11, which states:

> *And they had as king over them the angel of the bottomless pit, whose name in Hebrew is Abaddon, but in Greek he has the name Apollyon.*
>
> —Revelation 9:11

This verse tells us that Apollyon is the wicked angel of the bottomless pit and the king of the unleashed demonic "locusts"! Is it a coincidence that CERN has a statue of a Hindu god, Lord Shiva? Carrying a similar meaning behind the name Apollyon, Shiva also means the *god of destruction*, and is prominently displayed outside CERN. (Apollyon in Greek means *Destroyer.*)[9]

A few points of interest involving CERN's origins and agenda might be further understood when considering the following: The christianevidence .net article on May 31, 2019, lists nine points to consider regarding CERN.

1. ***The logo for CERN is three intertwined 6s, as in 666. There is no logical reason for this 666 pattern since the tunnels in CERN's facilities are not arranged like this. It begs the question, why?***
2. ***CERN is the birthplace of the World Wide Web (WWW).[10] Interestingly, the Hebrew equivalent of our "w" is the letter "vav" or "waw," which has the numerical value of 6. The English "www" transliterated into Hebrew is "vav vav vav" or 666.***
3. ***CERN derives its name from the horned god Cernunnos,[11] associated with the underworld. As mentioned earlier, the "bottomless pit" is associated with the underworld. It is also interesting that CERN conducts its "god" harnessing experiments deep underground.***
4. ***The machine at CERN has eight spokes/tubes radiating from its center, which resemble the occultic Wheel of Dharma.[12] Interestingly, CERN has named this structure "ATLAS." In the video series "Discourses on an Alien Sky#13,"[13] David Talbott suggests that the Cosmic Mountain associated with the Tower of Babel[14] was also represented by Atlas in Greek mythology. According to the myth, Atlas carried the weight of the heavens on his shoulders. ATLAS (A Toroidal LHC Apparatus) is also the name of an experiment at CERN.***
5. ***The acronyms CERN has used to title many of its experiments are demonic. These acronyms include SATAN (Solar Axion Telescopic ANtenna), which later had its name changed to CAST; DELPHI (DEtector with Lepton, Photon and Hadron Identification), which was a sanctuary of the god Apollo; and HADES (High Acceptance Di-Electron Spectrometer), which is the name of both the underworld and the god of the underworld.[15]***
6. ***On March 14, 2015, CERN released a strange occultic preview video titled "SYMMETRY." The video was filmed inside CERN and appears to contain at least some occult elements, which have nothing to do with the video's theme of finding the smallest particle. It has suggestions of rebirth, falling into an abyss, or even another plane of existence or time travel, and a dance dedicated to destruction before the resurgence. This weird, occult***

dance is highly significant because the large statue of Shiva sitting outside the CERN complex is seen performing this dance.

7. ***On June 1, 2016, the Gotthard Base Tunnel in Switzerland, the world's largest railway tunnel, marked its grand opening with an extremely bizarre, deeply occultic, satanic ceremony. Of significance is the fact that it occurred near CERN, also located over the area claimed to be the entrance to the underworld, and images that were projected on a massive video screen during the ceremony suggest a connection to CERN (e.g., the multi-armed Shiva doing the cosmic dance and the Atlas coming up out of CERN). The Gotthard ceremony featured a "goat-man" resembling Baphomet,[16] who dies, is resurrected, worshiped, and crowned as "the king of the world." In recent decades, Baphomet has become one of the key symbols used to represent Satan in the occult community. Other blatant occult references in the ceremony included the Eye of Providence,[17] prophecy, Lucifer, fallen angels, and more.***
8. ***On August 11, 2016, a bizarre leaked video surfaced of a satanic ritual human sacrifice taking place on the grounds of CERN in front of the Shiva statue. The video shows several individuals (unnamed scientists at CERN) in black cloaks gathering in front of the Shiva statue, in what appears to be a re-enactment of an occult ceremony, at the end of which a woman is stabbed. Whatever the intentions behind this ritual, the result is the same: It is yet another strange, ritualistic event associated with CERN.***
9. ***On June 24, 2016, peculiar "portal-shaped cloud formations" were photographed just above the LHC at CERN, coinciding with the initiation of a new "Awake" experiment by CERN scientists aimed at altering the particle collision process. Could it be possible that there was some connection between this new "Awake" experiment and these strange cloud formations? And precisely what do the researchers hope to "awaken" anyway?***[18]

On August 21, 2022, Elon Musk tweeted his thoughts about CERN on X/Twitter.[19] He sent this message: "Please let me use the CERN Large Hadron Collider. I am normal and can be trusted with a *demonic technology* unlike anything the world has ever seen."

Even if it is simply satire, it is a very dark satire. Could it be that Elon knows what is happening at CERN and wants to make a public statement about it?

IS CERN A SECOND BABEL?

> *Now the whole earth had one language and one speech.* [2] *And it came to pass, as they journeyed from the east, that they found a plain in the land of Shinar, and they dwelt there.* [3] *Then they said to one another, "Come, let us make bricks and bake them thoroughly." They had brick for stone, and they had asphalt for mortar.* [4] *And they said, "Come, let us build ourselves a city, and a tower whose top is in the heavens; let us make a name for ourselves, lest we be scattered abroad over the face of the whole earth."*
>
> —Genesis 11:1-4

CERN may be constructing a second dark tower. By the second tower, I am referring to CERN potentially being a follow-up, or sequel, to the first dark Tower of Babel as presented in Genesis 11. The parallel between Babel and CERN is fascinating in that the Tower of Babel was an attempt by humanity to step into realms they were not permitted to enter by God Almighty. As stated earlier, Babel's tower is considered by many to be much more than a structure reaching high into the heavens; it is viewed as a mechanism for reaching beyond our dimensional realm. Some believe God took action against what they were doing because the people of Babel and the Shinar valley were nearly successful in their endeavor. Reaching the heavens implies that they would open a portal for dark forces, potentially even the abyss mentioned in Revelation 9.

PARALLELS BETWEEN CERN AND THE TOWER OF BABEL

Here are some interesting parallels between CERN and the people of Babel in Genesis 11:

1. With its LHC, CERN might be attempting to reach into other dimensions, the spirit realm, or the heavens, just as the people of Babel wanted to construct a tower to reach the heavens (see Genesis 11:4).

2. CERN has created the largest structural mechanism ever, just as the people of Babel made the tallest building ever (see Genesis 11:4).
3. CERN created the World Wide Web to unite people under one language, and its project is a collaboration among 22 member states, just as the people of Babel spoke the same language and were united in their ambition (see Genesis 11:6).

Dark powers and all that is evil, including entities like CERN, represent the capabilities of this fallen world.

When considering this malfeasance, here is the good news: You are here! As part of the corporate body of Christ, the *Ekklesia.* Together, we are the restraining force in a world going mad. Elites and Luciferian-minded global leaders are driven like Nimrod to defy the ordinances and principles of the One True Living God and His Son, Jesus Christ.

Yet our presence defies all of their nefarious plans. The evil practices of those who would attempt to bring about a demonic force, even from the realm of the spirit, still cannot overcome the Church. Matthew 16:18 says, "And I also say to you that you are Peter, and on this rock I will build My church, and the gates of Hades shall not prevail against it."

Jesus told Peter that the gates of hell will not prevail against His *Ekklesia.* No system or force of evil can stand up to what Jesus declared over His Church, whether from this realm or the next. This means we are to enforce what He has given us by mixing the Word with our faith, doing the work of the kingdom, and being His Body in this natural world.

These evil powers can only prevail if we, the *Ekklesia,* stand back and passively allow them. Hebrews speaks of this: If His righteous one shrinks back, His soul has no pleasure in him.

> *Now the just shall live by faith; but if anyone draws back, My soul has no pleasure in him.*
>
> —Hebrews 10:38

This strong understanding suggests that when the empowered righteous shrink back from what God has given us to do, it grieves the Lord. Why? Because He has bestowed upon us all the power to combat and defeat these challenges. It doesn't matter how dire the situation becomes;

we are here, and the only way these evil devices will gain full power is if we step aside.

Sadly, many believers are not enforcing God's will on earth and are prematurely allowing far more than should be permitted. Nonetheless, we will still overcome the evil that seeks to rise in our day. Galatians 1:4 says, "Who gave Himself for our sins, that He might deliver us from this present evil age, according to the will of our God and Father."

There it is! God's will is that we be delivered from the present evil of our age and time. Take heart, neither CERN nor any other force that this natural world can conjure up will overcome the Word of God or His active Church! As long as the Church remains here and active, the full force and completion of the devil's plan to invade humanity by opening the abyss cannot be fully realized.

A WORD OF CAUTION

Now that we have examined the potential similarities between the Tower of Babel and the arguable modern equivalent, I would like to address the issue of good housekeeping. Throughout generations, many issues have arisen that were alarming. Yet, more often than not, all the predictions and ties to such scenarios have not materialized much of the way the prediction or sophisticated analysis suggested they might. A relevant consideration is the numerous predictions of the rapture occurring on a specific date, or the notion that Y2K was going to be a global event, sending us all back to the Stone Age. The same might be proven in time regarding CERN or future creations like it.

My purpose in writing this chapter is to prompt you to think and recognize the hour in which we are living. Fear and landing on absolutes is not my purpose. Years from the creation of CERN to the eventual replacement by another questionable technology may be the end result entirely. This was simply an examination of something culturally relevant that might give us a glimpse into a nefarious outcome.

However, dear reader, none of it may ultimately be what it appears to be. Your highest and best response is to stay in faith, although informed, not chasing conspiratorial trails that inevitably lead to more conspiratorial trails, seldom producing a positive outcome. Information is important, as long as it is in its proper place. My advice to you after examining these troubling points of interest is to remain in the Word of God.

I have a saying I often use—*gaze at God while glancing at the problem.* That is what David did when he fought Goliath. David's focus was not on Goliath but rather on his covenant with God Almighty. There is nothing wrong with examining what could be an issue of biblical proportions, but never should it be an obsession or fear. After all, everything involving CERN could ultimately turn out to be another conspiracy that merely distracts many, and in the end, it may result in nothing.

ADDITIONAL ISSUES ADDRESSED IN CHAPTER 14

In Chapter 14, I've expanded the list of agenda-driven issues facing society. Although it is not exhaustive, it is certainly informative. The purpose is to raise awareness so that you can pray, vote, or offer the foundation to make an informed response to many of these issues our children will face in the years to come. I encourage you to become acquainted with the issues listed in Chapter 14.

CHAPTER THREE

DEMON FORCES, CIVIC INSANITY, AND WESTERN SPIRITUALITY

RIGHTLY DISCERNING THE SPIRIT AND THE NATURAL

That which was from the beginning, which we have heard, which we have seen with our eyes, which we have looked upon, and our hands have handled, concerning the Word of life— 2 *the life was manifested, and we have seen, and bear witness, and declare to you that eternal life which was with the Father and was manifested to us.*

—1 John 1:1-2

John the Revelator, who also wrote the epistles of John, had to deal with various strange teachings in the early Church. These teachings question whether Jesus came in the flesh or had a physical body. Other teachers taught that the only way to enlightenment was through special knowledge. This is why John wrote in 1 John 1:1, "That which was from the beginning, which we have heard, which we have seen with our eyes, which we have looked upon, and our hands have handled, concerning the Word of life...." These verses address the issue of the day and refute the strange teachings circulating about Jesus.

COMPREHENDING SPIRITUAL MATTERS WITH WESTERN MINDS

Today, our natural world is what we experience every day, filled with the influence of demonic tormentors dedicated to bringing destruction to your life and those you love. Unfortunately, in our culture today, the spiritual world has not been at the forefront of the Western mind. The thought process in the Western mind resembles Greek thinking—logical and analytical. While this is not necessarily wrong, it creates a blind spot that dark forces can exploit.

Let me explain what I mean. In the days of the early Church (as mentioned in the previous section) and ancient history, the forces of spirits were prevalent and on most people's minds. It was easy to deceive many in the early Church through doctrinal fallacies, such as the aforementioned topics, including Gnosticism, Docetism, and other mystical, super-spiritual teachings. We can see this in 1 John, where John the apostle alludes to the issues of Gnosticism and Docetism and directs readers away from them.

The Book of 1 John indicates that the readers were confronted with the error of Gnosticism, which became a more serious problem in the second century. As a philosophy of religion, Gnosticism held that *matter is evil* and *spirit is good*. The solution to the tension between these two was knowledge, or *gnosis*, through which man rose from the mundane to the spiritual. In the gospel message, this led to two false theories concerning the person of Christ:

1. **Docetism**—regarding the human Jesus as a ghost
2. **Cerinthianism**—making Jesus a dual personality, at times human and other times divine.

The key purpose of 1 John is to set order to these issues affecting the early Church and to assure believers of their salvation.[1]

MASS IGNORANCE OF DARK SPIRITUAL FORCES

In our day, it has often been the opposite. Although we see mystical things and spiritual curiosity on the rise, spiritual forces in the Western persuasion have hidden behind the mass ignorance of their existence while displaying themselves through the culture. This display has come through the invasion of television entertainment and all the various forms of media we are constantly exposed to.

I've included a famous quote by commentator Paul Harvey regarding his thoughts on whether he was the devil.

"If I Were The Devil": A Warning to America from Paul Harvey

> ***"If I were the devil… If I were the Prince of Darkness, I'd want to engulf the whole world in darkness. And I'd have a third of its real estate, and four-fifths of its population, but I wouldn't be happy until I had seized the ripest apple on the tree—Thee. So I'd set about however necessary to take over the United States. I'd subvert the churches first—I'd begin with a campaign of whispers. With the wisdom of a serpent, I would whisper to you as I whispered to Eve: 'Do as you please.'***
>
> ***To the young, I would whisper that 'The Bible is a myth.' I would convince them that man created God instead of the other way around. I would confide that what's bad is good, and what's good is 'square.' And the old, I would teach to pray, after me, 'Our Father, which art in Washington….'***
>
> ***And then I'd get organized. I'd educate authors in how to make lurid literature exciting, so that anything else would appear dull and uninteresting. I'd threaten TV with dirtier movies and vice versa. I'd pedal narcotics to whom I could. I'd sell alcohol to ladies and gentlemen of distinction. I'd tranquilize the rest with pills.***
>
> ***If I were the devil I'd soon have families at war with themselves, churches at war with themselves, and nations at war with themselves; until each in its turn was consumed. And with promises of***

higher ratings, I'd have mesmerizing media fanning the flames. If I were the devil I would encourage schools to refine young intellects, but neglect to discipline emotions—just let those run wild, until before you knew it, you'd have to have drug-sniffing dogs and metal detectors at every schoolhouse door.

Within a decade I'd have prisons overflowing, I'd have judges promoting pornography—soon I could evict God from the courthouse, then from the schoolhouse, and then from the houses of Congress. And in His own churches I would substitute psychology for religion, and deify science. I would lure priests and pastors into misusing boys and girls, and church money. If I were the devil I'd make the symbols of Easter an egg and the symbol of Christmas a bottle.

If I were the devil I'd take from those who have, and give to those who want until I had killed the incentive of the ambitious.

And what do you bet I could get whole states to promote gambling as the way to get rich? I would caution against extremes and hard work in Patriotism, in moral conduct. I would convince the young that marriage is old-fashioned, that swinging is more fun, that what you see on the TV is the way to be. And thus, I could undress you in public, and I could lure you into bed with diseases for which there is no cure. In other words, if I were the devil I'd just keep right on doing what he's doing. Paul Harvey, good day."[2]

All the things Paul Harvey mentioned are occurring today and in many ways beyond. Another clever mechanism of the devil aligns with what Paul Harvey says and fits the spirit of the age: convincing the world that he doesn't exist.

"The greatest trick the Devil ever pulled was convincing the world he didn't exist."

—Charles Baudelaire[3]

POWER OF THE CHURCH

Today, there is a restraining force to this kind of nefarious activity—we, the *Ekklesia*, are here, and we, as the body of Christ, hold the full force of this kind of wickedness at bay from its full capacity. We are called to do what

Elisha did at Dothan in our time. Discern the realm of the spirit, know our authority, and begin to walk effectively to push darkness back and ultimately punish those same dark forces by our holy living, prayer life, and doing our assignment without wavering. When confronted with evil, we can take what the enemy thought would surround us, blind those forces, and give them the realization that they are the ones who are surrounded.

CIVIC INSANITY

On a smaller scale, regarding the free moral agency of individuals, the reality is that the devil and his dark forces influence the masses on a daily basis. What most people would dismiss as unhinged public behavior, or the extreme actions we observe under the label of activism, is often a demonic frenzy operating through the indoctrinated. Lacking any reference point for the devil and certainly none for God Almighty, these individuals gather in flash mob protests and outrage events. Their largely excused violent behavior has a common denominator—demon hosts driving the chaos of civic insanity.

The real force driving what is occurring within these individuals is a personality that is not their own. Demonic forces that have taken residence in an individual, along with others who are influenced by demons, will surge together. Those who succumb to this deception and the demonic power guiding them will act in unison until the final wave of disobedience is unleashed. One day, all those who worship themselves, and ultimately worship the devil through their reckless, godless behavior, will be the very catalyst that opens the pit mentioned in Revelation 9, unleashing hordes of spiritual beings from beyond the veil.

NAVIGATING SPIRITUAL WARFARE

For we do not wrestle against flesh and blood, but against principalities, against powers, against the rulers of the darkness of this age, against spiritual hosts of wickedness in the heavenly places.

—Ephesians 6:12

Understanding spiritual warfare is crucial for navigating today's world. There is significant hysteria and superstition surrounding this topic, making it essential to have ongoing, healthy teaching to maintain freedom in your mind and heart. With biblical knowledge, you are equipped to face what lies ahead, and most importantly, you can walk in revelation power. To be forewarned is to be forearmed. When under pressure, many people do not rise to the level of their potential; *they fall to the level of their training.* This principle greatly applies to spiritual warfare and much of what pertains to the supernatural realm.

There has been a significant amount of ineffective teaching on spiritual warfare. Understanding, liberation, and deliverance arise from knowing God's Word without the interference of unbelief, personal ideologies, superstitions, misunderstood Bible passages, or Hollywood films.

DEMON FORCES ARE VILE

You must know this: Demons are evil, murdering, vile, disgusting spirits that hate you, your family, and the Church of Jesus Christ. They know their time is short, and their goal is to destroy all of God's creation. Protection and freedom come from revelatory knowledge of God's Word and promises. When that knowledge is exchanged for the devil's lies, people experience bondage and difficulties.

MY DEMONIC ENCOUNTERS AT A YOUNG AGE

When I was very young, I often experienced dramatic demonic encounters. This had to do with the culture I was raised in, which included aspects of witchcraft and abuse. These encounters were not based on something I was doing wrong but on the gift of God's call for my life. Those occurrences created an entry point for evil spirits to run rampant in our home. My bed would shake at night, books would fall off my bookshelf, my TV would turn off and on, and I would see eyes in the window or an entity standing on the bed or walking around the room. I didn't know anything different, so I thought it was normal.

It was usual for me to walk outside and hear things being spoken. Some might think I needed some form of therapy. (Unfortunately, through misunderstanding this call of God, people can end up in mental institutions or places of difficulty because what's inside them gets corrupted through fear or the enemy's influence on their behavior.) I didn't realize in those days that sometimes what children encounter might point to them being spiritually sensitive to their environment.

I grew up in a culture of fear and have had these kinds of supernatural experiences my entire life. It wasn't until I came to the saving knowledge of Jesus Christ that I realized I was hypersensitive to the realm of the supernatural because I had a natural, DNA-born prophetic gift within me. You may have encountered similar things but don't understand how to explain them. What we need is Jesus Christ.

My journey began when I was born again and started embracing God's Word. I would read or listen to the entire New Testament once or twice a week. I sought to saturate my mind and emotions, aligning my thinking with God's Word. As I began to invest in the spirit, I started to reap benefits in the natural. Supernatural encounters became the norm for me. I would walk into places where worship was happening, and demons, being spirits, would sometimes shriek and cry out. They recognized the light of God I carried within me. Demon spirits cannot remain around a person who has the Word of God deeply rooted in their being. As a result, like anyone who becomes attuned to the Holy Spirit, my presence "demanded an explanation." Demons would flee, shackles would break off, and people would be set free.

FREE MORAL AGENTS

When God created us in His image, He gave us free will to do right or wrong, to serve or rebel, to be mighty weapons as sons and daughters for the living God or puppets for the devil. It all begins with what is believed, thought, and spoken. We are free moral agents who must daily choose whether we will follow God or be duped into believing the lies of the enemy. Demons don't have any power by themselves, but they can utilize a human vessel's power and authority.

Demons do not possess physical bodies. They cannot act unless they hijack the minds of free moral agents—human beings. People can surrender their power to the kingdom of darkness in various ways, including simple acts like dabbling in the occult (such as witchcraft, Ouija boards, astrology, etc.) or by believing the lies of the devil. Once control is relinquished to the enemy, the ability to guide lives toward God's ways is diminished or extinguished. This allows demonic entities to gain power and access to our natural world.

A person must grant permission for a demon to operate through them. By itself, a demon isn't scary, and neither is the kingdom of darkness. However, demons can be very persuasive, especially to an unsuspecting person who lacks a revelation and a relationship with the Lord Jesus Christ. That is why misunderstanding the Word of God is so dangerous.

CONSIDER THE SEVEN SONS OF SCEVA

Then some of the itinerant Jewish exorcists took it upon themselves to call the name of the Lord Jesus over those who had evil spirits, saying, "We exorcise you by the Jesus whom Paul preaches." [14] *Also there were seven sons of Sceva, a Jewish chief priest, who did so.* [15] *And the evil spirit answered and said, "Jesus I know, and Paul I know; but who are you?"*

—Acts 19:13-15

The sons of Sceva tried to cast out a demon, but they did not have the power of God behind their words because they were not fully persuaded that God had the power to do what He had promised. Demons know whether you are a believer or not.

These sons of Sceva were itinerant Jewish exorcists who had heard of Jesus after witnessing Paul cast out demons. Using the phrasing, "We exorcise you by the Jesus whom Paul preaches." They were reciting a "formula" based on what Paul said. Having no revelation of Jesus themselves proved to be powerless, the demon knew it, jumped up, tore off their clothes, gave them an epic beating, and sent them running naked and bleeding into the streets. That is the nature of the devil. His demonic characters will try to embarrass and destroy the body, the temple of God, because people are made in God's image.

ARE YOU FULLY PERSUADED?

Without weakening in his faith, he faced the fact that his body was as good as dead—since he was about a hundred years old—and that Sarah's womb was also dead. [20] *Yet he did not waver through unbelief regarding the promise of God, but was strengthened in his faith and gave glory to God,*

[21] *being* ***fully persuaded*** *that God had power to do what he had promised.* [22] *This is why "it was credited to him as righteousness."* [23] *The words "it was credited to him" were written not for him alone,* [24] *but also for us, to whom God will credit righteousness—for us who believe in him who raised Jesus our Lord from the dead.*

—Romans 4:19-24 NIV

A lack of knowledge and belief can allow areas of bondage and difficulty to occur. Many people do not have freedom because of what they believe, not what they think. Thinking transformed into believing is our goal. Being fully persuaded that what God says is true will give you a different kind of horsepower. Consider Abraham, as he was fully persuaded that God could bring forth a son even in his and Sarah's old age.

GOD AND THE DEVIL ARE IN A WAR FOR YOUR MIND

God is a Spirit, and those who worship him must worship him in spirit and in truth.

—John 4:24 KJV

Both God and the devil are territorial beings who are in a war for your mind. Whomever you give your mind to is who will eventually impact what you believe. You give your mind to God by reading His Word, praying, listening to worship music, walking out His will for your life, and acting upon His promises.

The devil is nothing compared to God. In the case of the kingdom of darkness, you place your mind on the things of this world and are led by your five senses—sight, hearing, smell, taste, and touch. This is called your "carnal mind" or "flesh" and is in direct opposition to God's Word, which says, "God is a Spirit" (*see* John 4:24), and "His Word is truth" (*see* John 17:17). As a child of God, you have a supernatural connection to Him through His Word. You need the grace of God, and you must worship Him in both spirit and truth.

The devil is also a spirit. Connecting with the devil on a spiritual level allows his lies to activate in your life. Both sides need a physical body to get things done on this earth. Spiritual warfare is God and the devil battling for your mind because it is the access point to your beliefs.

DARKNESS MAY WALK OVER BUT IT WILL GO LIMPING BACK

You could sink to the enemy's level simply by neglecting the Word of God. Which spirit will you allow to occupy the most space in your mind? This topic is fundamental. It's the birthplace of either spiritual victory or spiritual warfare. Whomever you give your mind to can determine the life you live today and the one you will live in eternity. The level of surrender to God or the devil dictates your level of victory.

You have a choice. Will you worship the living God and allow the truth of His Word to guide your life, or will you worship the god of this world and accept his lies? The devil's kingdom is one of darkness, while the kingdom of light belongs to God.

When you have a revelation of what God has for you, you become an unstoppable force. The power of God is calling to you at this moment. This is the season to stand firm and receive what the Lord has for you. The devil may send challenges your way, but with God, you can stand and say, "He can walk on over, but he's going to be limping back."

GOD AND THE DEVIL ARE NOT BUSINESS PARTNERS

> *Do not be unequally yoked together with unbelievers. For what fellowship has righteousness with lawlessness? And what communion has light with darkness?*
>
> —2 Corinthians 6:14

> *This is the message which we have heard from Him and declare to you, that God is light and in Him is no darkness at all.*
>
> —1 John 1:5

God and the devil are not business partners. Our Father cannot have fellowship with lawlessness or communion with darkness. Just as light does not tolerate darkness, the Lord Almighty does not tolerate the devil's presence.

The Lord God Almighty, who is light, only deals with darkness when you allow the devil into your life. That is why we need to inundate ourselves with His light. In 2 Corinthians 6:14, "light" refers to *knowledge* or *revelation* flowing from God's Word. Jesus is the Word made flesh (*see* John 1:14). Put the Word of God in you, and let it become a revelation of deep belief.

Believers who are fully persuaded of the truth of God's Word and have the light of God in them no longer expose their thinking to the kingdom of darkness or let it persuade their thinking. When you stand up to the war in your mind and push the devil back, you win in the areas where the devil's lies try to come against your finances, health, family, or depression. Whatever territory has the most space in your mind or your belief is what you will experience.

Jesus Christ is the Voice of God. Whatever Jesus is saying ALWAYS carries great authority.

ONGOING GOOD TEACHING IS THE BEST FORM OF DELIVERANCE

As His divine power has given to us all things that pertain to life and godliness, through the knowledge of Him who called us by glory and virtue.

—2 Peter 1:3

Through His Word, Jesus has already given you everything you need. The Bible tells us clearly to hate what God hates, but you can't do that if you don't have the Word of God alive in you. Both God and the devil are spirits. We are to worship God in spirit and truth (*see* John 4:24).

The thief does not come except to steal, and to kill, and to destroy. I have come that they may have life, and that they may have it more abundantly.

—John 10:10

God does not use the devil to achieve His purposes. God comes to give you life and life more abundantly. He doesn't use stealing, killing, and destroying to accomplish anything. This is so important to know! The highest form of deliverance is a revelation from ongoing, good teaching.

CHAPTER FOUR

POWER OF THE AIR AND BREAKING THE REBELLION OF WITCHCRAFT

In which you once walked according to the course of this world, according to the prince of the power of the air, the spirit who now works in the sons of disobedience.

—Ephesians 2:2

Popular misconceptions about spiritual warfare can be rightsized with a better understanding of scripture. Most spiritual warfare, simply put, is mind games. The fiery darts of the enemy try to get into your mind. They attempt to manipulate your emotions and influence your persuasion, willpower, thoughts, and decisions. However, the devil can't do anything unless he has humans, free moral agents, who surrender to his influence. When that happens, he has the power to do things in this natural world.

DIFFERENCES BETWEEN THE OLD AND NEW TESTAMENT

Suddenly, a hand touched me, which made me tremble on my knees and
on the palms of my hands. 11 *And he said to me, "O Daniel, man greatly*
beloved, understand the words that I speak to you, and stand upright, for
I have now been sent to you." While he was speaking this word to me, I

> *stood trembling.* [12] *Then he said to me, "Do not fear, Daniel, for from the first day that you set your heart to understand, and to humble yourself before your God, your words were heard; and I have come because of your words.* [13] *But the prince of the kingdom of Persia withstood me twenty-one days; and behold, Michael, one of the chief princes, came to help me, for I had been left alone there with the kings of Persia.* [14] *Now I have come to make you understand what will happen to your people in the latter days, for the vision refers to many days yet to come."*
>
> —Daniel 10:10-14

There's a big difference between the Old Testament and the New Testament. Knowing the difference is essential in spiritual warfare. People dealt with the devil, or the kingdom of darkness, differently in the Old Testament than in the New Testament. There is understanding in this that will open the eyes of your understanding, and you will find you have a lot more authority and ability than you ever thought you did. This is especially powerful for believers in Jesus Christ. You are an absolute challenge to the kingdom of darkness based on what you know. The Word of God teaches us that people are destroyed for a lack of knowledge (*see* Hosea 4:6); what you don't know can hurt you.

DIFFICULTIES WITH PRINCIPALITIES

Daniel 10 discusses difficulties with principalities, real demonic forces, in angelic warfare. Daniel received a message from God in a vision. He fasted and prayed for three weeks for an answer before the encounter with an angelic being occurred.

Please take note: Daniel prayed, and his prayers were immediately heard. In other words, from the moment his words were spoken, they were heard, and action took place. But there was resistance in the heavenlies, and it took three weeks before he received an answer.

In understanding this process, you've learned in the New Testament that Jesus said, "...for the prince of this world cometh, and hath nothing in me" (*see* John 14:30 KJV). We also know Jesus taught us through the Word of God that the prince of this world, Satan, is now being cast out. In the Old Testament, the devil and all his demonic authority were accessible in the heavens to the presence of God and humanity.

In the New Testament, a change has occurred. Jesus died on the cross and was resurrected. The situation where demonic entities fought against the messengers of God in the Old Testament is very different from the New Testament. In the Old Testament, angels had to travel a great distance and fight through all the hordes of hell to convey a message to someone like Daniel. In the New Testament, when we pray, God, the Hope of Glory, has given us His Holy Spirit, who now lives within us. He's as close as our next breath.

PRINCE OF THIS WORLD BEING CAST OUT

It was very different for Daniel. He didn't have the Holy Spirit in him. He had to call on God and get angels to punch through the hordes, whose opposition was direct angelic warfare. In the New Testament, when Jesus said the prince of this world (and his demonic hordes) were being cast out (*see* John 12:31 KJV), it meant they could no longer hold back the messengers of God. It's a supernatural Spirit-to-spirit message between God and man.

There are still angelic things that happen. The only difference between then and now is that demonic entities can only function through free moral agents (people) in the New Testament age. Demons have to get hold of your mind to cause you to agree with them. Demonic entities cannot rise and take over circumstances and regions without people who have thinking minds coming into agreement with the devil.

Preaching the gospel is the number-one form of spiritual warfare. When we stand up in Jesus' authority, we cut through the powers of darkness. The war is not only supernatural but also a war of mind renewal.

WHAT ABOUT THE PRINCE OF THE POWER OF THE AIR?

And you He ***made alive****, who were dead in trespasses and sins,* [2] *in which you* ***once walked*** *according to the course of this world, according to the prince of the power of the air, the spirit who now works in the sons of disobedience,* [3] *among whom also we all once conducted ourselves in the lusts of our flesh, fulfilling the desires of the flesh and of the mind, and were by nature children of wrath, just as the others.*

—Ephesians 2:1-3

People who think in line with the devil typically allow him to function at a great capacity in this natural world. But we who have the kingdom of God within us enforce God's kingdom by preaching the Word and casting out demons.

People have told me, "That's all well and good, Joseph, but what about the passage in the Bible that talks about the 'prince of the power of the air still works in the sons of disobedience'? Isn't there a demon prince flying around causing all kinds of trouble? How do we deal with that?"

It is essential to recall that Ephesians 2:1-3 is a New Testament scripture. In verse 1, Paul reminds us He (Jesus) *made* (past tense) *alive* us who were *once* (no longer) dead in trespasses and sins because we *walked* (past tense—we no longer walk) according to the natural world, using our five senses only. Because He died for our sins and rose again, we have been *made alive* in Him with all the benefits of our salvation.

HIGH PLACES

Ephesians 2:2 mentions "the prince of the power of the air, the spirit who now works in the sons of disobedience." Many people focus on the word "air." In the Old Testament, there were "high places," mountaintops, where the "sons of disobedience," the pagans, worshiped their gods and sacrificed children, animals, etc., to them. This pagan idol worship angered God, and He commanded the Israelites to destroy the *high places.*

> *Then you shall drive out all the inhabitants of the land from before you, destroy all their engraved stones, destroy all their molded images, and demolish all their **high places**.*
>
> —Numbers 33:52

> *You shall utterly destroy all the places where the nations which you shall dispossess served their gods, on the **high mountains** and on the hills and under every green tree.*
>
> —Deuteronomy 12:2

Combine these verses with 2 Corinthians 10:5 about every "high thing" that must be cast down. This includes thinking patterns, strongholds, and bondages, as well as anything that contradicts the truth of God's Word.

Casting down arguments and every ***high thing*** *that exalts itself against the knowledge of God, bringing every thought into captivity to the obedience of Christ.*

—2 Corinthians 10:5

There is a popular opinion that takes the scripture from Ephesians 2:2, which talks about the *prince of the power of the air,* then combines it with the Old Testament concept about the *high places* on mountains, where the kingdom of darkness was worshiped and torn down by good kings, and then combines it with 2 Corinthians 10:5 where we are to be obedient to tear down the *high thing.*

Thus, a spiritual warfare community has been created that believes the *high places* must be the geographically high-altitude spots on the earth, such as mountains, electric, cell, and radio towers, satellites, and flying airplanes. They have determined this is where they must wage war against demonic forces, the *sons of disobedience* (demons) who live and operate in these high-altitude geographic areas. This doctrine is wrong based on the New Testament Greek definitions of the word "air."

TWO GREEK WORDS; TWO DIFFERENT MEANINGS

In which you once walked according to the course of this world, according to the prince of the power of the ***air****, the spirit who now works in the sons of disobedience.*

—Ephesians 2:2

There are two ancient Greek words used for "air." The first, *aether*, describes *high, thin, clean air.* It means *high altitude*, like a mountain. When people read about high places in the Scripture, they think the high place must represent physically high-altitude places and be where the demons live. They've mixed the Old Testament version of the high places with a New Testament understanding of the *prince of the power of the air.* That's when people conclude that the devil controls radio waves, TV signals, satellites, mountains, etc. Many people believe they need to climb radio towers, mountains, or get in an airplane to do warfare and speak to dark entities in "high" places.

Unfortunately, people who combine the scriptures about air and high places misunderstand their meaning. That's why it is essential to understand the Greek in these instances. *Aether* is not the Greek word used for air in Ephesians 2:2. It's not about high altitude, thinner, cleaner air up by the tops of mountains.

The Greek word for "air" in the verse is *aér.* This word for air refers to *a low altitude, the lower dense region of the air.* The high places discussed in the Old Testament have nothing to do with a geographical location, such as high up in the mountains, in the clouds, or in thinner, higher air.

In some commentaries, *aér* references roughly six feet off the ground, close to where the average human mind is when standing. When you put this together with all the other scriptures we've shown that have to do with taking thoughts captive and putting things under the authority of Jesus—the devil goes around like a roaring lion seeking whom he may devour (*see* 1 Peter 5:8)—you realize the devil is fighting for control of your mind, which is about six feet off the ground.

MIND CONTROL

Both God and Satan are fighting over who controls your thoughts and emotions. That's why understanding the truth of Ephesians 2:2 is so essential. Again, it is not saying demonic entities are swarming and flying high up in the atmosphere. No. There's nothing up there for the kingdom of darkness except thin, clean air. The hordes of hell that are fighting to get control of your mind and the minds of the masses are walking around in low-altitude, dense-air places.

Whoever controls the mind, the thinking process, controls the direction people go. Just think what happens when you get several people thinking in line with the prince of the power of the air. It establishes the kingdom of darkness.

> *For the kingdom of God is not eating and drinking, but righteousness and peace and joy in the Holy Spirit.*
>
> —Romans 14:17

The kingdom of darkness is also a persuasion that first affects the mind and then flows outward into the "eating and drinking" natural world. The prince of the power of the air is talking about the kingdom of darkness established in a mind or a group of people's minds. Unless people think in line with Satan's plan, he cannot establish his plan for this natural world. That's why the devil has false preachers and false prophets and uses persuasion to influence thoughts.

> *And do not be conformed to this world, but be transformed by the renewing of your mind, that you may prove what is that good and acceptable and perfect will of God.*
>
> —Romans 12:2

Romans 12:2 teaches not to conform to the mindset of the prince of the power of the air but to be transformed by renewing your mind to God's perfect will. To summarize, there are no demonic strongholds in the physical sky. The air it's talking about is the mind.

THE MIRROR AND YOUR SENSES

> *For we know in part and we prophesy in part.* [10] *But when that which is perfect has come, then that which is in part will be done away. ...* [12] *For now we see in a **mirror, dimly**, but then face to face. Now I know in part, but then I shall know just as I also am known.*
>
> —1 Corinthians 13:9-10, 12

The natural refers to what is happening in our natural persuasion or human experience within this natural world. The spirit is the God part of us. Between the natural and the spiritual, there is what could be called a veil or a "mirror, dimly."

The human experience is not necessarily a God experience. But it is what most people are led by—our five senses: seeing, hearing, smelling, tasting, and touching.

> *...that is, those who by reason of use have their senses exercised to discern both good and evil.*
>
> —Hebrews 5:14

We must exercise our senses by using them. We must employ them to discern between good and evil, what is natural and what is of the spirit. You exercise these senses by renewing your mind with the Word of God to affect the realm of the spirit. The more you discipline your five senses, the more you put yourself in order with the Word of God.

Your soul is the determining factor here. It is the dividing line or the veil between the natural and the spirit. Your soul is composed of your mind, will, and emotions. It is essential to be aware of and in control of your soul. Don't let your emotions run away with you because when you do, you allow your five senses to dominate your experience. The natural will dominate the spirit in your experience, and you'll be giving your mind to the kingdom of darkness or the prince of the power of the air. Instead, you need to renew your thoughts and employ your will by disciplining your five senses to the Word of God. Then true power happens. The result is that the devil cannot affect you, and you can influence society or these lower denser regions of the earth by preaching the gospel, casting out demons, and driving back the prince of the power of the air. Keep your soul in check for greater power.

That's not to say we don't pray! We can push these things back and strip the power and effectiveness of evil powers leveraging human minds. We engage in prayer and spiritual warfare because our weapons are powerful in God, capable of destroying the effects of free moral agents who are ungodly and allow the devil to work through them. Through prayer, we are mighty in God against the effects of witchcraft, offense, and every evil and terrible thing that is happening all around the world.

DEMONS' UNAUTHORIZED POWER

We're not just taking on the devil. We're taking on people who have authorized the devil to have power over their mindset. When you pray, you strip that mindset of its power and potency, making you more effective in your space.

Here's an example. Witches and ungodly people have attended meetings where I have ministered. They are completely surrendered to the devil, and they meditate on the devil the same way a believer would meditate on the Bible. It's not only the fact that the devil has overtaken their lives and they have given their minds, emotions, and behaviors over to the kingdom of darkness, but it's also the fact that they have come into my airspace. There's a supernatural confrontation when their darkness comes into contact with my light. I wrestle, not with flesh and blood, but against evil powers and principalities (*see* Ephesians 6:12). If a true believer stands in front of someone fully persuaded by the devil, the result is that demons are driven out.

REBELLION AS WITCHCRAFT

A particular element associated with deception is rebellion. In today's culture, rebellion is often encouraged and viewed as a positive trait. The statement, "*Rebellion* is as the sin of witchcraft," gets quoted often, but it may not be fully understood. Let's briefly examine the following scripture reference and what this means in greater depth.

> *So Samuel said: "Has the LORD as great delight in burnt offerings and sacrifices, as in obeying the voice of the LORD? Behold, to obey is better than sacrifice, and to heed than the fat of rams.* [23] *For rebellion is as the sin of witchcraft, and stubbornness is as iniquity and idolatry. Because you have rejected the word of the LORD, He also has rejected you from being king."*
>
> —1 Samuel 15:22-23

When taking this scripture into context, we can ascertain a definition for the phrase, "Rebellion is as the sin of witchcraft." First, we need to recognize that rebellion is a violation of authority.

VIOLATION OF AUTHORITY

In the case of Saul and Samuel, it was a violation of God's authority. But how is this tied together with witchcraft? The answer is man's will over God's will. When a person prioritizes their desires or actions over what God has instructed, it is an act of rebellion. Regarding spiritual things, acts of rebellion are defined by a person who wants to access the realm of the spirit by their own means.

Behavior such as this is tragic. Saul attempted to play it off; however, God was not pleased. Later, we see Saul stepping into witchcraft by engaging with the witch of Endor to pull Samuel up from the grave. Saul's action fulfilled what he started when he disobeyed Samuel's words, "To obey is better than sacrifice." The following is the account of Saul's encounter with the witch of Endor.

THE WITCH OF ENDOR

*Now **Samuel had died,** and all Israel had lamented for him and buried him in Ramah, in his own city. And Saul had put the mediums and the spiritists out of the land.* 4 *Then the Philistines gathered together, and came and encamped at Shunem. So Saul gathered all Israel together, and they encamped at Gilboa.* 5 ***When Saul saw the army of the Philistines, he was afraid, and his heart trembled greatly.*** 6 ***And when Saul inquired of the LORD, the LORD did not answer him, either by dreams or by Urim or by the prophets.*** 7 ***Then Saul said to his servants, "Find me a woman who is a medium, that I may go to her and inquire of her." And his servants said to him, "In fact, there is a woman who is a medium at En Dor."***

8 *So Saul disguised himself and put on other clothes, and he went, and two men with him; and they came to the woman by night. And he said,* ***"Please conduct a séance for me, and bring up for me the one I shall name to you."*** 9 *Then the woman said to him, "Look, you know what Saul has done, how he has cut off the mediums and the spiritists from the land. Why then do you lay a snare for my life, to cause me to die?"*

10 *And Saul swore to her by the LORD, saying, "As the LORD lives, no punishment shall come upon you for this thing."* 11 *Then the woman said, "Whom shall I bring up for you?" And he said, "Bring up Samuel for me."* 12 ***When the woman saw Samuel, she cried out with a loud voice. And the woman spoke to Saul, saying, "Why have you deceived me? For you are Saul!"*** 13 *And the king said to her, "Do not be afraid. What did you see?" And the woman said to Saul, "I saw a spirit ascending out of the earth."*

14 *So he said to her, "What is his form?" And she said, "An old man is coming up, and he is covered with a mantle." And Saul perceived that it was Samuel, and he stooped with his face to the ground and bowed down.* 15 ***Now Samuel said to Saul, "Why have you disturbed me by bringing me up?"*** *And Saul answered, "I am deeply distressed; for the Philistines make war against me, and God has departed from me and does not answer me anymore, neither by prophets nor by dreams. Therefore I have called you, that you may reveal to me what I should do."*

> 16 *Then Samuel said: "So why do you ask me, seeing the LORD*
> *has departed from you and has become your enemy?* 17 *And the LORD*
> *has done for Himself as He spoke by me. For the LORD has torn the*
> *kingdom out of your hand and given it to your neighbor, David.* 18 *Because*
> *you did not obey the voice of the LORD nor execute His fierce wrath*
> *upon Amalek, therefore the LORD has done this thing to you this day.* 19
> *Moreoever the LORD will also deliver Israel with you into the hand of the*
> *Philistines. And tomorrow you and your sons will be with me. The LORD*
> *will also deliver the army of Israel into the hand of the Philistines."*
> 20 *Immediately Saul fell full length on the ground, and was dreadfully*
> *afraid because of the words of Samuel. And there was no strength in him,*
> *for he had eaten no food all day or all night.* 21 *And the woman came to*
> *Saul and saw that he was severely troubled, and said to him, "Look, your*
> *maidservant has obeyed your voice, and I have put my life in my hands*
> *and heeded the words which you spoke to me."*
>
> —1 Samuel 28:3-21

Saul had gone from disobeying Samuel to fully exercising witchcraft! An interesting thought is that just as the servant had a quick answer about where to find a witch, many are ready to assist someone in unintentionally disobeying God! Watch who you surround yourself with!

UNAUTHORIZED ACCESS TO THE REALM OF THE SPIRIT

Witchcraft is unauthorized access to the realm of the spirit. Those who do not obey authority in the natural and those who disobey on a spiritual level are the same. Both are unauthorized violations of authority.

> *But even if we, or an* ***angel from heaven****, preach any other gospel to you than what we have preached to you, let him be accursed.*
>
> —Galatians 1:8

Many things could occur regarding those who claim things they likely have not truly seen or experienced. Here are three that you may find helpful over the years.

1. **Fake encounters:** Simply experiences contrived by misguided people's imagination, desiring the experience more than the truth.
2. **Self-deception:** As unique as it may sound, through my experiences with the prophetic, I have seen a profound need for people to be validated; they often imagine encounters and call them real. It's almost as if they give themselves to their imagination and call it visions, dreams, etc.
3. **Demonic encounters:** Demonic persuasion or experiences involving agents from the kingdom of darkness having access to the mystical through ignorance.[1]

HOW SHOULD THE BELIEVER RESPOND?

Ultimately, self-discipline by the Word of God is the highest form of combating demonic forces. A person committed to being a living sacrifice through self-denial and a solid biblical foundation is primed to have an explosive and highly effective prayer life. Without having the mechanism of your thoughts and emotions, along with your belief system, under the control of the Word of God, followed by the leading of the Holy Spirit, the results will be diluted and weak.

A fully trained and operational believer is required to combat all the elements of surprise attacks by darkness and the current world. This does not mean perfection; what it means is dedication. To be a disciple is to be a disciplined follower of Jesus Christ. If a person claims to be a disciple of Jesus, they must be an active follower of Jesus' teachings and the realities of the New Covenant.

A potent force for God is released through this kind of believer. You are called to be that kind of believer. Loyal to the Lord Jesus Christ and available at His call.

Dear reader, I believe that is who you are. Now, you must believe it and become that living sacrifice, which is your reasonable service unto the King (*see* Romans 12:1). Remember, in it all, Jesus loves you, and there is nothing you can do about it. You might as well marshal your life to follow Him, build your discernment, and walk in the Spirit.

SECTION 2

STRATEGIES OF THE DEVIL AND THE RESPONSIBILITIES OF THE BELIEVER

CHAPTER FIVE

SATAN'S RAGE

Therefore rejoice, O heavens, and you who dwell in them! Woe to the inhabitants of the earth and the sea! For the devil has come down to you, having great wrath, because he knows that he has a short time.

—Revelation 12:12

Wrath is the native mode of the devil. He knows his time is short and his fury is aimed at man, God's precious creation. Why does Lucifer hate humankind? It was possibly due to Lucifer observing the timeline in heaven. Everything was moving along smoothly for him. He was likely the anointed musician in heaven. He was also known as the anointed cherub who covers (*see* Ezekiel 28:14). Then God, the Father, created Adam, and the devil saw that Adam was made in the likeness and image of God. This man, Adam, was the "first Adam," the son of God created directly by the Father, who gave him dominion over the earth. Everyone who would be born on Earth came through the first Adam.

When Lucifer saw God breathe life into man, jealousy, followed by rage, filled his heart. Because of this, war broke out as Lucifer began to explain to many angels that God had demoted them from their "rightful place." Michael, the warring archangel, gathered angels faithful to God the Father and collided with the rebellious horde of angels who went rogue.[1]

LUCIFER'S FALL

How you are fallen from heaven, O Lucifer, son of the morning! How you are cut down to the ground, you who weakened the nations! [13] *For you have said in your heart: "I will ascend into heaven, I will exalt my throne above the stars of God; I will also sit on the mount of the congregation on the farthest sides of the north;* [14] *I will ascend above the heights of the clouds, I will be like the Most High."* [15] *Yet you shall be brought down to Sheol, to the lowest depths of the Pit.*

—Isaiah 14:12-15

Lucifer was arrogant, prideful, and ambitious. His desire to exalt himself above the Lord God Almighty caused his forced exit from heaven.

Michael and his angels cast them out of their access to heaven. Thus began the saga of light versus darkness, with humankind in the balance. The epic levels of violence, atrocities, and evil experienced throughout history stem from this moment. It is sad to realize that God did not create Adam to endure such things. He was made for fellowship, for family. When the Lord walked with Adam in the cool of the day, He built a relationship with Adam. His plan was never to see evil come upon creation or on His son and daughter, Adam and Eve. The good news is that God was not outmatched and cannot be outwitted. Jesus would come one day as the Last Adam and change everything.

LUCIFER'S CONTEMPT

Of judgment, because the ruler of this world is judged.

—John 16:11

Lucifer's contempt was something he had birthed in his heart from the beginning of his existence. In John 8:44, Jesus called the devil "a murderer from the beginning" and "the father of liars." In the Book of Revelation, John the apostle clarifies that the dragon mentioned is "that serpent of old," also known as the devil or Satan.

So the great dragon was cast out, that serpent of old, called the Devil and Satan, who deceives the whole world; he was cast to the earth, and his angels were cast out with him.

—Revelation 12:9

He laid hold of the dragon, that serpent of old, who is the Devil and Satan, and bound him for a thousand years.

—Revelation 20:2

The devil led a conflict that erupted among the angelic ranks within heaven's armies, and it was all over humanity. It is a fascinating thing to consider that these angelic beings believed Lucifer over God to the point that war erupted. This has often led me to ask, "Why would God allow this? How is it that these angels could think in this fashion?" Students of the Word of God can get glimpses of why the devil was so angry.

Let's consider a passage from Job 1, in which Satan comes before God among the "sons of God." The term "sons of God" is derived from the Hebrew word *b'nai Elohim,* implying that these *angels are God's direct creations.* This refers to the angels present before God's throne. The same reference is used again in Job 38:7, when *the sons of God shout for joy at the creation of the world.*

Angels enjoyed the status of being direct creations of God the Father Himself. There was nothing like them until He created the first man. Adam was also a direct creation of God, but that is not all! Adam was made in God's image and likeness because he had the very breath of God within him! This set him apart from the angels who, although they were themselves direct creations of God, did not carry His image and likeness as Adam did. As a result, this may have been the main point the devil used to accuse God to the angels who believed his lies.[2]

Satan knows his ultimate destination, and this knowledge has fueled his fury. This knowledge has reverberated throughout history, beginning with Eve's temptation in the Garden of Eden. Through the devil's deceit, Adam forfeited his authority, which allowed Satan to become the ruler of the earth.

And the dragon was enraged with the woman, and he went to make war with the rest of her offspring, who keep the commandments of God and have the testimony of Jesus Christ.

—Revelation 12:17

Do you not know that the saints will judge the world? And if the world will be judged by you, are you unworthy to judge the smallest matters? [3]

> *Do you not know that we shall judge angels? How much more, things that pertain to this life?*
>
> —1 Corinthians 6:2-3

Your understanding of God's Word is vital in spiritual warfare. The devil knows he is a defeated foe and is terrified that you will figure it out. First Corinthians 6:2-3 points to his fear. Paul was talking to the people of Corinth and asking them why they were disputing with one another. In verse 3, Paul asks, "Do you not know that you shall judge angels?" Think about the power of that phrase. Angels are beneath you, and demons are fallen. You are far above them in the rank and file of authority in all of creation in the universe. The angels you will judge are the fallen angels preserved until Christ's return. Here's a verse to back that up:

> *And the angels who did not keep their proper domain, but left their own abode, He has reserved in everlasting chains under darkness for the judgment of the great day.*
>
> —Jude 1:6

I believe these fallen angels, including Satan, who "did not keep their proper domain," are going to be judged by believers in Jesus Christ.

KEEP THE WORD OF GOD THE MAIN THING

Go to the Word of God regarding what I am about to say. Keep the main thing the main thing. Whenever we take steps into arenas of speculation, we mustn't force an issue and do what biblical studies label *eisegesis*—basically, the idea that a person injects their ideas, beliefs, and philosophies into the text of Scripture rather than extracting what the Scripture is saying. This doesn't mean we cannot or should not consider looking into the possibilities. This is exactly what we will do when looking into the following scripture.

Ezekiel 28 references what many scholars would agree is a passage regarding the devil. Let's read the following reference and consider the possibilities.

> ***You were in Eden****, the garden of God; every precious stone was your covering: the sardius, topaz, and diamond, beryl, onyx, and jasper, sapphire,*

> *turquoise, and emerald with gold. The workmanship of your timbrels and*
> *pipes was prepared for you on the day you were created.* 14 *You were the*
> *anointed cherub who covers; I established you; you were on the holy moun-*
> *tain of God;* ***you walked back and forth in the midst of fiery stones****.* 15
> *You were perfect in your ways from the day you were created, till iniquity*
> *was found in you.*
>
> 16 ***By the abundance of your trading*** *you became filled with violence*
> *within, and you sinned; therefore I cast you as a profane thing out of the*
> *mountain of God; and I destroyed you, O covering cherub, from the midst*
> *of the fiery stones.* 17 *Your heart was lifted up because of your beauty; you*
> *corrupted your wisdom for the sake of your splendor; I cast you to the*
> *ground, I laid you before kings, that they might gaze at you.* 18 *You defiled*
> *your sanctuaries by the multitude of your iniquities, by the iniquity of your*
> *trading; therefore I brought fire from your midst; it devoured you, and I*
> *turned you to ashes upon the earth in the sight of all who saw you.* 19 *All*
> *who knew you among the peoples are astonished at you; you have become*
> *a horror, and shall be no more forever.*
>
> —Ezekiel 28:13-19

First of all, it reads "You were in Eden." This cannot be talking about anyone else but Lucifer. Only three individuals were present in Eden: Eve, Adam, and the serpent. Now, there is much conjecture about the serpent. I take the conventional view that the serpent is indeed Lucifer, now becoming Satan, because Adam and Eve gave him their position and seat of authority.

Second, notice it says, "You walked back and forth in the midst of the *fiery stones*." Some have suggested this may refer to the planets in our solar system.

Third, Ezekiel tells us iniquity was found in Lucifer. How? By the abundance of his trading. Why would it say, "the abundance of his trading"? It is possible that before the fall, he was handling commerce on Earth, and the moment humanity was created, he realized his position as the cherub who oversaw or covered this planet (or all the planets, also known as "the stones of fire") was suddenly diminished. Lucifer was being put out of a job. Jealousy and rage took over, which caused him to rebel and destroy all of God's new rulers of Earth from Eden.

Fourth, Lucifer was cast down, as the remainder of the reference above in Ezekiel 28 states. Jesus, of course, makes mention of this moment:

> *And He said to them, "I saw Satan fall like lightning from heaven.* [19] *Behold, I give you the authority to trample on serpents and scorpions, and over all the power of the enemy, and nothing shall by any means hurt you."*
>
> —Luke 10:18-19

Jesus says, "I saw Satan fall like lightning." His powerful statement regarding the devil being cast out, but then adds, "I give you authority to trample on serpents and scorpions and over all the power of the enemy, and nothing shall by any means hurt you."

In the exact moment, Jesus tells the disciples that He witnessed Satan's fall. He continues by placing that instance in the same category as the authority we have been given over snakes, scorpions, and all the power of the enemy. Again, He might be referencing when these fallen angels, their demon cohorts, and all the power they collectively possessed likely fell to earth with Satan. Demons themselves were likely added to the mix later on. A fierce battle over Earth may be because all these evil and dark forces have no other place to influence except Earth![3]

When Jesus arrived on Earth, He disrupted their free rein on the planet. He set the precedent by being the firstborn among many brethren. First, Jesus had to come and lay the groundwork for us. Jesus is the "Last Adam" and is also directly from the Father, who was born of God. Jesus, who was entirely God, agreed to become fully man. He came to Earth to take back what Adam had lost. Jesus had to be born of water or have a natural birth to take authority as a Man before He could give that authority to His Church.

THOSE BORN OF WATER HAVE AUTHORITY

> *There was a man of the Pharisees named Nicodemus, a ruler of the Jews.* [2] *This man came to Jesus by night and said to Him, "Rabbi, we know that You are a teacher come from God; for no one can do these signs that You do unless God is with him."* [3] *Jesus answered and said to him, "Most assuredly, I say to you, unless one is born again, he cannot see the Kingdom of God."* [4] *Nicodemus said to Him, "How can a man be born when he is old?*

> *Can he enter a second time into his mother's womb and be born?"* [5] *Jesus answered, "Most assuredly, I say to you,* ***unless one is born of water and the Spirit, he cannot enter the kingdom of God.*** [6] *That which is born of the flesh is flesh, and that which is born of the Spirit is spirit."*
>
> —John 3:1-6

John 3:1-6 helps us understand what was needed for Jesus to accomplish His mission. Notice that Jesus told Nicodemus one must be born of *water* and the *Spirit* to enter the kingdom of God. This terminology, *water* and *Spirit,* is about a person being born of a woman into the natural world. The water breaks, and a baby is born. Jesus Himself had to be born of a woman into this natural world, as any other entrance would have been illegal! In Jesus' explanation to Nicodemus, we see that a person must have a physical body to carry authority in this world. Without a physical body or being born into this world, a person cannot be born of the Spirit or saved.

The Spirit is the God-breathed part of Jesus, the Word, but He did not have a physical body in heaven; He was not flesh. Why was this important? Adam had a physical human body, which was required to have authority and dominion over the earth. Therefore, Jesus could not enter the world with only His Spirit entity. To become fully man, Jesus needed to be born of a woman, *born of water.*

WHAT TOOK SO LONG?

> *And I will put enmity between you and the woman, and between your seed and her Seed; He shall bruise your head, and you shall bruise His heel.*
>
> —Genesis 3:15

God could not just *make* Jesus be born. Prophecies needed to be written, spoken, and accepted for that to happen. The Spirit is the Word throughout the Old Testament, leading up to Jesus' birth. God prophesied that Jesus would bruise Satan's head as early as the time of the first Adam.

The Old Testament prophets needed to speak in faith throughout history. David, Isaiah, and many others prophesied Jesus' birth. When enough things were spoken into the atmosphere by faith, the Spirit of God, or the

Word, culminated in what was necessary to manifest in the natural. Finally, the Holy Spirit could hover over Mary and ignite the seed, the Word of God, within her. Jesus began to grow in Mary's womb until her water (born of water) broke, and the human baby Jesus was born on the earth. He became the "Last Adam."

BORN OF THE SPIRIT

And when He had said this, He breathed on them, and said to them, "Receive the Holy Spirit."

—John 20:22

To enter the kingdom of God or be "born again" (*see* John 3:3-5), you need not only to be born of water through a woman—you must be born again in the Spirit and reunited with God.

Jesus did that for His disciples when He visited them after His resurrection. Jesus breathed on them and said, "Receive the Holy Spirit." For salvation and to enter God's kingdom, you first need a physical body, then the Holy Spirit. Notice what happens when you are *born of water* and the *Spirit.*

There is therefore now no condemnation to those who are in Christ Jesus, who do not walk according to the flesh, but according to the Spirit. [2] *For the law of the Spirit of life in Christ Jesus has made me free from the law of sin and death.* [3] *For what the law could not do in that it was weak through the flesh, God did by sending His own Son in the likeness of sinful flesh, on account of sin: He condemned sin in the flesh,* [4] *that the righteous requirement of the law might be fulfilled in us who do not walk according to the flesh but according to the Spirit.*

—Romans 8:1-4

ONE BELIEVER IS ENOUGH TO ROUT THE FORCES OF HELL

Jesus is the firstborn among many brethren and came to "condemn sin in the flesh." He became flesh and lived among us to defeat the devil at his own game—to take back what had been stolen and return his dominion over the earth to man. If just one believer were left on the planet, that believer would have more authority than all the powers of darkness combined. Jesus Christ is Lord, and He's in you. You have a physical body; the devil doesn't.

As a free, moral, physical bodied, Spirit-filled agent, you can conquer any demonic attack that rises against you. The only place Satan and his demons can wage war against you is in your mind. The battle for the mind is to gain access to the decision-making part of people's hearts and minds so the devil can hijack a physical body.

You can cast a demon out of a person because a demon does not belong there, but you cannot cast the Holy Spirit out of a person because the Holy Spirit makes you one in spirit with God the Father. You have a physical body and the right to make Jesus Christ the Lord and ruler over your physical body and unite your spirit to Him in salvation. When you get a revelation that He has given you the power to choose good or evil, you can win in spiritual warfare just by showing up. Your voice coming from your physical body, as a chariot for the presence of God in the natural world, repels and casts out demons, pushes back the powers of darkness, and drives them out.

You have authority over your family, business, and ministry in all you do and everywhere you walk. Jesus is Lord over your circumstances because you're born of the Spirit and water. Get this revelation, and you'll have raw, overcoming, yolk-busting horsepower to cut down the spiritual forces of wickedness in heavenly places.

Remember, the devil hates humanity because God favored humanity over Lucifer. Pride, ambition, and greed on Lucifer's part came to the forefront when he recognized that we were being elevated above him. Jesus, through His work on the cross and resurrection, settled the issue once and for all, as He is the firstborn among many brethren—we who are in Christ. Not only are humans in general given a higher place than the devil, but as believers, we additionally have power and authority over him. Rage and a volcanic hatred are the only things Satan has due to being defeated by Jesus. Thank God that *greater is He who is in us than he that is in the world!*

CHAPTER SIX

CONQUERING THE DEVIL'S GAMES

Remember, God and the devil are neither buddies nor business partners. God does not like the devil, and the devil does not like God. They do not work behind the scenes to put deals together for the greater good of society. Satan was cast out of heaven, and Jesus saw him fall like a bolt of lightning to the earth.

> *And he said unto them, I beheld Satan as lightning fall from heaven.*
>
> —Luke 10:18 KJV

Jesus' purpose for coming to the earth was to destroy the works of the devil.

> *He who sins is of the devil, for the devil has sinned from the beginning. For this purpose the Son of God was manifested, that He might destroy the works of the devil.*
>
> —1 John 3:8

> *The thief does not come except to steal, and to kill, and to destroy. I have come that they may have life, and that they may have it more abundantly.*
>
> —John 10:10

Jesus brought about the greatest breakthrough in history. As we see in 1 John 3:8 and John 10:10, the war is no longer in heaven. Satan has been cast down to the earth, where he is working to steal, kill, and destroy God's creation. Jesus has met him in battle here on earth to obliterate and destroy the devil's plans and to make a way of escape for us through His death and resurrection. He can't stand the devil or his works.

> *Inasmuch then as the children have partaken of flesh and blood, He Himself likewise shared in the same, that through death He might destroy he who had the power of death, that is, the devil.*
>
> —Hebrews 2:14

Just before Jesus went to the cross, He told His disciples that the ruler of this world, Satan, is judged for the world's fallen state, and it is time for his reign and ownership of this earth to end. He will be dethroned and "cast out."

> *Now is the judgment of this world; now the ruler of this world will be cast out.*
>
> —John 12:31

JESUS FULFILLED HIS PURPOSE

> *I will no longer talk much with you, for the ruler of this world is coming, and he has nothing in Me.*
>
> —John 14:30

The enemy, Satan, the ruler of this world, has nothing in Jesus. Jesus, the light of the world, triumphs over darkness. Satan has no foothold or authority over Jesus.

JESUS PUNISHED THE DARK POWERS

Jesus came to destroy the power of death and the grave. The devil lied, deceived Eve in the Garden of Eden, and took Adam's authority. Jesus' death and resurrection disarmed and triumphed over Satan and his cronies and took back that authority once and for all. Then, He made a public spectacle of them.

Having disarmed principalities and powers, He made a ***public spectacle*** *of them, triumphing over them in it.*

—Colossians 2:15

Kings of old would first disarm their adversaries by taking their weaponry away from them. These victorious kings would make a gruesome *public spectacle* of their captured enemies. Defeated foes would have their eyes gouged out and their tongues, right thumbs, and big toes cut off. They were stripped naked and paraded through the streets in chains. This humiliating parade showed they had been rendered useless and powerless in every area of life. They had become entirely subservient, like a slave or a servant.

Jesus did that to the kingdom of darkness, and I believe He did it in the realm of the unseen, in front of Abraham's bosom. He showed the devil as a defeated foe to all the hordes of hell, the armies of heaven, and the saints of old who were in paradise. He paraded them in the most powerful and embarrassing way known to man.

The foundation of spiritual warfare is predicated on the revelation of what Jesus did to them and what He gained for us.

Behold, I give you the authority to trample on serpents and scorpions, and over all the power of the enemy, and nothing shall by any means hurt you.

—Luke 10:19

Satan is a defeated foe. Jesus won back our authority over the earth! Once again, we have power over snakes and scorpions, which is all the power of the enemy. A revelation of what Jesus did in the realm of the spirit will make you a terrorist to the kingdom of darkness.

THE DEVIL IS ALLOWED ACCESS

But I fear, lest somehow, as the serpent deceived Eve by his craftiness, so your minds may be corrupted from the simplicity that is in Christ.

—2 Corinthians 11:3

As a result of Jesus' victory, the only place the devil has access to you is your mind. He can influence your thoughts; if he can, he will again have power in the natural world. The war is for your mind.

Remember Eve in the Garden of Eden? The serpent (Satan), who deceived her with his craftiness, attacked Eve in her mind. Her mind was corrupted.

ABIDE IN JESUS

> *I am the vine, you are the branches. He who abides in Me, and I in him, bears much fruit; for without Me you can do nothing.*
>
> —John 15:5

Jesus wanted us back so much that He came to destroy the devil at his own game. As long as we remain and abide in Him and His words abide in us, we destroy the devil in any area of our mind. We need Jesus!

If we do not abide in Him, stay in His Word, and operate in His truth, we may be susceptible to the same temptation that corrupted Eve's mind. Now that he has been defeated, the devil's goal is to take your focus off the Word and corrupt the simplicity of what is found in Christ. The apostle Paul says:

> *For I am jealous for you with the jealousy of God himself. I promised you as a pure bride to one husband—Christ. [3] But I fear that somehow your pure and undivided devotion to Christ will be corrupted, just as Eve was deceived by the cunning ways of the serpent. [4] You happily put up with whatever anyone tells you, even if they preach a different Jesus than the one we preach, or a different kind of Spirit than the one you received, or a different kind of gospel than the one you believed.*
>
> —2 Corinthians 11:2-4 NLT

FORGIVENESS OUTFLANKS OFFENSE

> *Now whom you forgive anything, I also forgive. For if indeed I have forgiven anything, I have forgiven that one for your sakes in the presence of Christ, [11] lest Satan should take advantage of us; for we are not ignorant of his devices.*
>
> —2 Corinthians 2:10-11

Yes, Satan is a defeated foe in the spirit, but the war in the mind is to bring offense to you. If he can bring offense to you and get you into unforgiveness, then he has a foothold in your mind.

Paul explains why walking in forgiveness is so important in spiritual warfare. We must not be ignorant of his strategies. He is defeated in the spirit, but we are free moral agents and have physical bodies. We are in charge of our minds. He has power in the natural world only when people give him access. He can't do it without permission. If Satan can bring offense and turn doubts, unbelief, or fear into unforgiveness, we have given him an inroad. Satan is an "evil genius" who wants to tamper with our minds for his purposes.

MIND GAMES

In 2 Corinthians 2:11, another Greek word for "devices" is *noēmata,* which can include *mind games*. The devil plays shrewd and devious games. His strategy is to attack and make human beings victims. His primary tactic involves leading us into offense, which can lead to unforgiveness. This unforgiveness gives him access to our lives, allowing him the freedom to influence us. This influence can result in severe torment in our minds, and in extreme cases, it may even lead to insanity.

For example, a friend tells you about a conversation they overheard that may or may not pertain to you, but you assume they were talking negatively about you behind your back. You repeatedly replay what you heard from your friend until you've created several possible scenarios of what the conversation could be about. Without talking to the people in the original discussion, you become irritated with them. How dare they say things like that about you! Your imagination runs away with these thoughts, and you become offended. The next time you see them, it looks like they are ignoring you as they walk by (on the other side of the street), and you become even more offended. The devil has used a *mind game* against you. Do you let him win this battle? NO! As a child of God, you become aware of this tactic!

Once you are "not ignorant of his devices," you'll know what he is up to and can take action to stop him in his tracks. When you don't give in to being offended and instead exercise forgiveness, it's over for the devil. You have not given him an inroad to your mind because forgiveness breaks spiritual wickedness and influences your life.

That's why Jesus said to the disciples, "I do not say to you, up to seven times, but up to seventy times seven" (*see* Matthew 18:22). Shut down the devil's mind games. Forgive and keep a pure heart—even if you're right. Forgiveness is powerful against the kingdom of darkness; it is the key to victory in spiritual warfare.

A well-known saying is, "Unforgiveness is like drinking poison and hoping someone else dies." The point of forgiveness is not to release the other person. It's to set you free. Agree with Jesus, who destroyed the works of the devil. You can overcome every onslaught the devil brings against your mind.

Jesus loves you, and there's nothing you can do about it. He destroyed the devil's work in the spirit and the natural, but He needs you to keep offense out of your mind by walking in forgiveness and love.

> *Be sober, be vigilant; because your adversary the devil walks about like a roaring lion, seeking whom he may devour.*
>
> —1 Peter 5:8

Love and forgiveness are weapons of warfare that shut down the mouth of the roaring lion.

PHYSICAL BODIES OUTRANK DEMON SPIRITS

> *Then God said, "Let Us make man in Our image, according to Our likeness; let them have dominion over the fish of the sea, over the birds of the air, and over the cattle, over all the earth and over every creeping thing that creeps on the earth."*
>
> —Genesis 1:26

You are the Father's masterpiece, and when you understand your value in Him, you realize He has already put everything in place for you to overcome any enemy attack. You're made in the image and likeness of God. This is why the devil comes to steal, kill, and destroy (*see* John 10:10). He wants to hurt those made one step lower than God, His creation. That's what spiritual warfare is all about.

For You have made him a little lower than the ***angels****, and You have crowned him with glory and honor.*

—Psalm 8:5

Yet You have made him a little lower than **God,** *and You crown him with glory and majesty!*

—Psalm 8:5 NASB

In the New King James version of the Bible, the Hebrew word for "angels" is *Elohim.* In the first five chapters of Genesis, the word *Elohim* refers to *the supreme God.* Early translators had difficulty expressing that man was just a little lower than the one and only God, so they used the word "*angels*" instead. (You can check the version of your Bible. If you have a center or side reference column, it will say the word for angels is *Elohim.* In other versions, like the NASB, the translators have kept the original meaning of *Elohim* intact.)

In the rank of authority of the universe, it goes like this: God, man, angels, animals, bacteria, pond scum, and then demons. Anything with a physical body in the natural has more authority than a demon. This truth is powerful! The very fact that you have a physical body gives you more authority than a demon.

You are a son or daughter of the living God.

I will be a Father to you, and you shall be My sons and daughters, says the LORD Almighty.

—2 Corinthians 6:18

You are seated with Him in heavenly places:

Even when we were dead in trespasses, [He] made us alive together with Christ (by grace you have been saved), [6] *and raised us up together, and made us sit together in the heavenly places in Christ Jesus.*

—Ephesians 2:5-6

You are as He is in this world:

> *Love has been perfected among us in this: that we may have boldness in the day of judgment; because as He is, so are we in this world.*
>
> —1 John 4:17

You are a joint heir with Christ:

> *And if children, then heirs—heirs of God and joint heirs with Christ, if indeed we suffer with Him, that we may also be glorified together.*
>
> —Romans 8:17

You are no longer a servant but a friend of His:

> *No longer do I call you servants, for a servant does not know what his master is doing; but I have called you friends, for all things that I heard from My Father I have made known to you.*
>
> —John 15:15

You have been given authority and power:

> *Behold, I give you the authority to trample on serpents and scorpions, and over all the power of the enemy, and nothing shall by any means hurt you.*
>
> —Luke 10:19

You have direct access to God, and He calls you family. We are direct descendants of Jesus Christ, the firstborn among many brethren (*see* Romans 8:29). We have His authority, strength, and ability. What a powerful thing to be in Christ Jesus with His Word working in us.

God has an attitude toward the devil. He wants him destroyed and thrown out of your life. The only thing allowing the devil into your life is you. How you think, read the Word (or not), and manifest thoughts can open the door to him. It is your responsibility to transform your mind and reject the devil.

CHAPTER SEVEN

THE BATTLE FOR YOUR MIND

A spiritual war is taking place. There are supernatural evils, difficulties, and fights, and you need a solid foundation of knowledge and revelation to know how to battle in the spirit. Supernatural evils exist, but we will follow the biblical model for effective breakthroughs in spiritual warfare.

SATAN'S TEMPTATION OF JESUS

> *Then Jesus, being filled with the Holy Spirit, returned from the Jordan and was led by the Spirit into the wilderness,* [2] *being tempted for forty days by the devil. And in those days He ate nothing, and afterward, when they had ended, He was hungry.* [3] *And the devil said to Him, "If You are the Son of God, command this stone to become bread."* [4] *But Jesus answered him, saying, "It is written, 'Man shall not live by bread alone, but by every word of God.'"*
>
> —Luke 4:1-4

Satan used food as his first temptation because he knew that Jesus was weak with hunger. That's one of the devil's tactics—come at us when we are weakest.

Food is the same temptation Satan used with Eve in the Garden of Eden. He asked, "Did God say you would surely die if you eat this?" (See Genesis 3:1-4.) The question was designed to bring doubt and unbelief into her mind about what she knew. This battle in the mind is spiritual warfare. It's not just demons; it is mind warfare. It's challenging to fight if you don't understand the tactics, but it becomes very powerful once you do.

IT IS WRITTEN

Satan also assaulted Jesus' identity. "*If* you are the Son of God...." You should be able to turn this stone into bread. In other words, prove who You are. Even in His human weakness, Jesus countered this temptation with the Word of God. "It is written...."

> *Then the devil, taking Him up on a high mountain, showed Him all the kingdoms of the world in a moment of time.* [6] *And the devil said to Him, "All this authority I will give You, and their glory; for this has been delivered to me, and I give it to whomever I wish.* [7] *Therefore, if You will worship before me, all will be Yours."*
>
> —Luke 4:5-7

The first temptation did not work, so the devil offered Jesus all the kingdoms of the world. Satan was tempting Jesus with control of the earth and the worship and glory of the people. The devil wasn't lying about his authority over the earth. That's why Jesus did not rebuke him for it. It was a fact.

THE DEVIL WAS OFFERING JESUS A SHORTCUT

Somehow, supernaturally, in a moment, Satan was able to give Jesus a revelation of all the kingdoms of the world. This vision could be taken in a couple of different ways. Satan could have shown Him the epochs or other times in history, or it could have been a simultaneous vision of seeing all the world's kingdoms suddenly in His Spirit. The devil tempted Jesus with the very reason He came—to redeem us and establish His kingdom in the second coming. Jesus knew the first Adam was deceived and forfeited it to him. The devil had the authority to give the earth to whomever he wished. He offered Jesus a shortcut by providing the world to Him. All Jesus had to do was bow down and worship Satan.

> *And Jesus answered and said to him, "Get behind me Satan! For it is written 'You shall worship the LORD your God and Him only you shall serve.'"*
>
> —Luke 4:8

The point is that if you have a supernatural encounter, you should ensure it aligns with God's Word.

> *Then he brought Him to Jerusalem, set Him on the pinnacle of the temple, and said to Him, "If you are the Son of God, throw Yourself down from here. [10] **For it is written**: 'He shall give His angels charge over you, to keep you,' [11] and, 'in their hands they shall bear you up lest you dash your foot against a stone.'"*
>
> —Luke 4:9-11

In the first two temptations, Jesus countered the devil by using the Word of God: "It is written...." So, for the third temptation, Satan decided to try to deceive Jesus with scripture. The devil knew to quote this because he was angelic in origin and knew what God's Word said about him and his kind. But the devil quoted scripture out of context and contradicted what God says in the rest of scripture. Jesus countered this temptation with the truth of scripture.

JOB'S TEMPTATION

Satan tempted Jesus for the second time by offering him all the kingdoms of the world, as he had authority over them. This authority was granted to him when he deceived Adam and Eve. Consequently, Adam relinquished his authority over the earth to Satan. Because of this, the devil could do whatever he wanted with the earth.

In Luke 10:18, Jesus said, "I saw Satan fall like lightning from heaven." This must have happened earlier in history. Why? Because in the Book of Job, the devil was able to come into the presence of God with the sons of God.

> *Now there was a day when the sons of God came to present themselves before the LORD and Satan also came among them.*
>
> —Job 1:6

When he was in heaven, the devil was called Lucifer, but the Lord Jesus called him Satan. This means that after he had fallen, was cast out, and became Satan, he was able to come before God. Satan now had Adam's position in his dominion. Adam used to walk with God in the cool of the day and had total access to God. He was able to be with the Lord. Adam and Eve were sent out of the garden after Adam gave his authority to the devil.

Then, there was a day when the sons of God came to present themselves before the Lord, and Satan came among them. Notice the Lord didn't say, "I cast you out. What are you doing back here?"

Instead:

> *And the LORD said to Satan, "From where do you come?" So Satan answered the LORD and said, "From going to and fro on the earth, and from walking back and forth on it."*
>
> —Job 1:7

At this time, there was no serious covenant between God and man, not in the same way that Adam had it or the same way Jesus established it. What you see here between God and His relationship with humanity is a "do the best you can" scenario. It was a dispensation with no written law for Job to follow. (Job pre-dated Moses' receipt of the law.) God still loved humankind and saw Job as a righteous man who would not fall for the devil's tricks and lies. This explains why God pointed him out to Satan.

> *Then the LORD said to Satan, "Have you considered My servant Job, that there is none like him on the earth, a blameless and upright man, one who fears God and shuns evil?" 9 So Satan answered the LORD and said, "Does Job fear God for nothing? 10 Have You not made a hedge around him, around his household, and around all that he has on every side? You have blessed the work of his hands, and his possessions have increased in the land. 11 But now, stretch out Your hand and touch all that he has, and he will surely curse You to Your face!" 12 And the LORD said to Satan, "**Behold**, all that he has is in your power; only do not lay a hand on his person." So Satan went out from the presence of the LORD.*
>
> —Job 1:8-12

In other words, Satan can't take his life because death and life are in the power of his tongue (*see* Proverbs 18:21). Notice the word "behold" in verse 12. The Hebrew word for "behold" is *hinnēh,* meaning *behold*, or *look, now*. It often expresses strong feelings, such *as surprise, hope, and expectation,* thus giving vividness depending on its surrounding context.[1] In Hebrew, this is the equivalent of God saying, "Hey, Satan, surprise, all he has is in your hands."

I don't think the devil knew what he had gained when Adam turned his authority over to him because of the word "behold," or *surprise*. Once he obtained the earth from Adam, Satan had the power to attack Job. I believe the devil didn't realize what he had because he had such contempt for God's creation that he disregarded what he had gotten from them. He so devalued humankind that he did not realize the extreme value God had placed on Adam by giving him authority.

A MORE OPPORTUNE TIME

> *And Jesus answered and said to him, "It has been said, 'You shall not tempt the LORD your God.'"* [13] *Now when the devil had ended every temptation, he departed from Him until an opportune time.*
>
> —Luke 4:12-13

After Satan was finished tempting Jesus, he departed from Him until *an opportune time*. That opportune time came when Jesus told the disciples what He must do.

> *From that time Jesus began to show to His disciples that He must go to Jerusalem, and suffer many things from the elders and chief priests and scribes, and be killed, and be raised the third day.* [22] *Then Peter took Him aside and began to rebuke Him, saying, "Far be it from You, Lord; this shall not happen to You!"* [23] *But He turned and said to Peter,* ***"Get behind Me, Satan! You are an offense to Me,*** *for you are not mindful of the things of God, but the things of men."*
>
> —Matthew 16:21-23

Satan spoke through Peter. Here, the devil was again trying to tempt Jesus through a friend in an effort to keep Him from the cross. It might be startling to realize that the devil can work through acquaintances who may be using logic and compassion, but really, it is a device to take you off track. Peter was the devil's access point for a more *opportune time.*

In Luke 4:12, Jesus says, "You shall not tempt the LORD your God." The Greek word for "tempt" is *ekpeirazo*, equivalent to "test." It means *don't test God by forcing His hand or making Him display His power through frivolous actions* like jumping off the top of the temple.

THERE IS ONLY ONE PLACE WE CAN TEST THE LORD

According to the Word of God, there's one place you can test Him, and that's by your giving and receiving (*see* Malachi 3:10). What you cannot do is test His power through a thoughtless activity that has no fruit in it. For example, the Bible says you have authority over venomous snakes and scorpions. It does not tell you that you should snatch up one for show, saying, "I'm going to let this snake bite me to show you it can't hurt me because God will take care of me." That's testing God.

But if, like Paul, one were to bite you when you picked up a bundle of sticks to throw on a fire, you would suffer no harm (*see* Acts 28:3-5). If you are a true believer, God is there to enforce His Word. You must be in line with the Word of God. That's how Jesus overcame every temptation of the devil—through the Word of God.

SATAN'S ARSENAL

Luke 4:13 says, "Now when the devil had ended every temptation, he departed from Him." There were only three temptations mentioned, but this seems to be the total of the devil's temptation arsenal. In the various temptations, Satan tried to cause Jesus to fall through hunger, identity, power, and authority, and identity again. Isn't that what the devil tries with God's people as well? Let Jesus be your example of overcoming temptation through the Word of God. You have the same authority to overcome everything the enemy throws your way.

THE FOCAL POINT

It is essential for you to delve deeper into the Word of God. Realize that where demons come from and how they operate is not the most important thing. The focal point is that you have the authority to tread on snakes and scorpions and all the enemy's power (*see* Luke 10:19). In context, snakes and scorpions refer to demons.

A person who has a physical body, whether you're born again or not, can resist demons. You can starve demons out with willpower, even if you're not born again. This is one of the reasons why people get rid of addictions when they don't know God. They're free moral agents, and the power of choice and willpower can still stop the devil. How much more so the sons and daughters of God who give their lives to Jesus! Jesus positioned us to take the world back. That's why we need to win people to Jesus.

THE NATURAL WORLD WAS NOT MADE FOR SPIRITS

This world was not made for spirits. It was made for bodies. Only people, human beings, born into this world can be born again (*see* John 3:5-7). Many people teach a doctrine that even Satan could be born again. This is a false doctrine. He cannot because he's not a physical creature. He's only a spirit; spirits can't be saved without being born into this world. It's also why angels can't be saved.

THE ULTIMATE ACT OF SPIRITUAL WARFARE

> *Then I heard a loud voice saying in heaven, "Now salvation, and strength, and the kingdom of our God, and the power of His Christ have come, for the accuser of our brethren, who accused them before our God day and night, has been cast down."*
>
> —Revelation 12:10

The ultimate act of spiritual warfare is to win someone to Jesus Christ and pull them out of darkness into light. They can enforce the kingdom of God with willpower, the power and authority given to them through Jesus' death and resurrection. Both God and the devil are territorial, and they want access to your mind. Only you can give it to them. Through your choices, you are the deciding factor in that narrative.

The devil had access to the presence of God in Job 1 because he stole Adam's authority. But Jesus came as the last Adam and drove him out. Through Jesus, we can fight off the effects of the devil's tactics.

JESUS INTERCEDES FOR US

> *Therefore He is also able to save to the uttermost those who come to God through Him, since He always lives to make intercession for them.*
>
> —Hebrews 7:25

Jesus is our great intercessor. When the devil shows up to accuse the brethren, he runs into our big Brother—the Firstborn among many brethren, the Son of God, the First and Last who was and is to come, the Prince of Peace, the King of Glory, and the Righteousness of God. He is seated at the right hand of God. So when the devil shows up to accuse a believer, he may have walked in, but he will be limping back!

If the devil accuses you, he is accusing Jesus. As He is, so are we in this world (*see* 1 John 4:17). Jesus Christ is Lord. If you're in Him and His Word abides in you when the devil accuses, it's like he's accusing the Son of God to the Father, and neither will hear it.

THE DEVIL EATS DIRT

The devil cannot come directly against you because Jesus intercedes for believers. Instead, he will try to get you to do his old job. He wants you to accuse and cut down the brethren. It's his greatest temptation to have you cut down your brothers and sisters, so you hold offense over them.

It doesn't matter if you're right. If you're holding offense, you open a playground for the devil. He will introduce you to sin, sickness, and all kinds of nefarious, sinful things, even though you are redeemed from all of it. This is spiritual warfare.

What are his tactics? How does he influence you to step outside what you know to be true from the Word of God?

> *Be sober, be vigilant; because your adversary the devil walks about like a roaring lion, seeking whom he may devour.*
>
> —1 Peter 5:8

First Peter 5:8 is a powerful scripture. Why is it using the word "sober"? Because it's talking about your thinking. Let's parallel that scripture with Genesis 3:14.

> *So the LORD God said to the serpent: "Because you have done this, you are cursed more than all cattle, and more than every beast of the field; on your belly you shall go, and you shall eat dust all the days of your life."*
>
> —Genesis 3:14

The serpent (the devil) was cursed to crawl on its belly. Notice that the verse also says that the serpent's food is the dust of the earth. Snakes crawl on the ground, but they don't eat dirt. It might look like it with their tongues, but they're not eating dirt. They eat other stuff, but this is about the devil, not snakes. The *devil* will eat the dust of the earth. What was Adam's body made from? The dust of the earth.

First Peter 5:8 says, "Be sober." It means you are to be sober in your thinking. In other words, be aware that the devil is always looking for someone he may devour. But notice it says he's like a "roaring lion." The devil can't jump out of the bushes and devour you. He's *seeking whom he may devour.* What is it he can devour? According to Genesis 3:14, he can only eat dust. The dust represents our flesh because Adam's flesh was made of dust. The *roaring* is him using his voice to shake your sober thinking and bring fiery darts into your mind so he can have access to your body.

DON'T SURRENDER TO HIS VOICE!

> *In the sweat of your face you shall eat bread till you return to the ground, for out of it you were taken;* ***for dust you are****, and to dust you shall return.*
>
> —Genesis 3:19

The devil can only devour what you surrender, and if you are not "sober-minded" with the Word of God, he will "roar" like a lion to shake you and gain access to your mind. He can influence your thinking through offense, fear, illness, financial issues, relationship problems, or any other factor that disrupts your life if you are not vigilant. Once you start focusing your thoughts on any of these things, he will roar louder and bring more negative, unbiblical thoughts to your mind.

He will devour part of your life if you're not vigilant in the fight against his roar and stand up with the Word. You may find yourself more deeply offended or face a difficult challenge due to illness or financial struggles. These thoughts shake your sober thinking rooted in God's Word. At that point, the serpent is devouring your carnal (flesh) mind. Just as God told Adam and Eve when they exited the garden, they were created from dust. The devil eats dust.

THE SHIELD OF FAITH

Above all, taking the shield of faith with which you will be able to quench all the fiery darts of the wicked one.

—Ephesians 6:16

Many people try to fight the devil with their carnal ideas. That's like fighting a rabid wolf and trying to hold it off with a bloody piece of steak. Instead, the Word of God must be used.

The shield of faith allows you to withstand the fiery darts of the enemy, which are your thoughts, persuasions, and offenses. If you're letting offenses or strife in, you are participating with the accuser of the brethren. You're allowing the fiery darts of the enemy to get past your shield of faith, which is the Word of God. You wonder why there's chaos in your life, why you don't feel right. It's because you are in a spiritual warfare.

Casting down arguments and every high thing that exalts itself against the knowledge of God, bringing every thought into captivity to the obedience of Christ.

—2 Corinthians 10:5

Take every thought captive with the shield of faith, and it will stop the fiery darts of the enemy with the authority of Jesus Christ. Be ready to punish every disobedient thought that does not line up with God's Word. You can talk to your brain and emotions and say, "I'm not letting offense get me.

Nope. I will not be an agent for the kingdom of darkness. I will not be an accuser of the brethren. I will not allow unresolved issues to penetrate my mind." It is vital to wash your mind with the Word of God.

BECOME RE-SENSITIZED TO THE HOLY SPIRIT

Many are in deep need of becoming re-sensitized to the Holy Spirit because they have been *traumatized by religion*. Extended times of worship and prayer are necessary for this to occur.

In my younger years, I would lead and participate in extended times of worship and prayer. We would worship for hours. As a youth pastor, many years ago, my entire focus was to introduce young people to the presence of God. A saying we often used, and still do today, goes like this: "Five minutes in the presence of God can do more than five years of therapy." Presence-based living creates power-based children. It was true then, and it is true today! Being in a culture of worship and the presence of God causes individuals to live differently. An awareness of who God is and the weight of His glory profoundly affects the human experience. It makes alterations that cannot be completed any other way.

RETURN TO THE FOUNDATION

We live in a culture where the *generals of the faith* and many historical biblical heroes are largely forgotten. I'm reminded of Exodus 1:8, which speaks of a new king who came into power "who did not know Joseph." Even though this great man of God rescued the people and helped them become a strong nation, they had no memory of him. If we do not understand the foundation of something or how it was established, we are likely to disrespect or disregard it.

The absence of discipline, guidance, heroes, and the presence of God regularly causes an internal fight that brings insecurity and confusion. What are we to do to answer this fight, both within ourselves and in others? We need to cultivate an encounter with God! That's the prescription!

Humanity was not created to solve these issues. No process in the human experience solves internal or external problems without substances, relationship crutches, the pursuit of money, or all the familiar "go-tos."

An encounter with God is desperately needed, which only comes through those who have been with Him. An amazing thing happens when the fight inside is answered. The *peace that passes understanding* will rise (*see* Philippians 4:7), confusion will leave, and joy will grow in place of your former experience. It must be said that *the human experience is not a God experience!* To experience this peace, you must flood your mind and emotions with His Word, increase worship, and enter God's presence. Suppose an individual is not reading the Bible, praying, or spending time in worship and fellowship with God. In that case, they shouldn't be surprised when they are depressed, cast down, sick, fearful, broken, confused, and all the other sad issues that so many are subjected to without His protection. Only God can answer the fight inside, but to encounter God, there must be exposure to His presence and His people.

Prayer and intercession are a direct result of those who know the presence of God.

> *...The effective, fervent prayer of a righteous man avails much.* 17 *Elijah*
> *was a man with a nature like ours, and he prayed earnestly that it would*
> *not rain; and it did not rain on the land for three years and six months.* 18
> *And he prayed again, and the heaven gave rain, and the earth produced*
> *its fruit.*
>
> —James 5:16-18

"The effective, fervent prayer of a righteous man avails much." What a statement!

"Effective, fervent" is the Greek word *energeō*:

1. To be operative, be at work, put forth power, to work for one, aid one.
2. To effect.
3. To display one's activity, show one's self-operative.

This tells me that we should pray with intentional power, working in prayer until we receive a release or see a breakthrough. We should be aggressive in prayer and speak boldly when necessary!

The following is the same passage, which is found only in the Amplified version:

> *...The heartfelt and persistent prayer of a righteous man (believer) can accomplish much [when put into action and made effective by God—it is dynamic and can have tremendous power].*
>
> —James 5:16 AMP

To step into effective, fervent prayer, there must be a return to a love for the Word of God. No Word, no faith; no faith, no effective praying. This is an area of great concern in the Church today; many in this upcoming generation have only a little grasp, if any, of the Bible. As a result, the question of what is right and what is wrong promotes a convoluted topic in today's society.

Additionally, we are being drawn into a culture war. It is a war over ideals, and it will affect the very souls of our children's children. Many before us fought for a better tomorrow, only to see the present generation disregard their sacrifices. The responsibility lies at the feet of a weak Church and a permissive society that has allowed the lawless, Antichrist spirit to run wild.

> *Where there is no revelation, the people cast off restraint; but happy is he who keeps the law.*
>
> —Proverbs 29:18

Fist-shaking or cursing the darkness has never been a productive response when dealing with a brainwashed culture. The best response is to point to something magnificent—a future of hope and a seemingly impossible vision of what we could have. I want to remind the people of God where they come from and what *could be* if they only stand up and take it! This begins with an encounter with the Living God. Prayer and times of worship are essential to awaken a generation.[2]

CHAPTER EIGHT

UNLOCK THE SPIRITUAL REALM

Now faith is the substance of things hoped for, the evidence of things not seen.

—Hebrews 11:1

For since the creation of the world His invisible attributes are clearly seen, being understood by the things that are made, even His eternal power and Godhead, so that they are without excuse.

—Romans 1:20

There is a spiritual reality and a natural reality. Effectiveness in a Spirit-filled life is understanding how to draw out what is in the realm of the Spirit and see it manifest in the natural. Romans 1:20 supports the reality of God's invisible qualities, such as His eternal power and divine nature, and all His attributes in the realm of the Spirit, which are seen and understood from what has been made. This implies that the natural world provides evidence of the supernatural.

However, the spiritual is not first, but the natural, and afterward the spiritual.

—1 Corinthians 15:46

First Corinthians 15:46 refers to the bodies of Adam and Jesus, one being natural and the other originating from the Spirit. When considering this scripture, I one day began to recognize the reality of the realm of the spirit and the necessary steps required to receive what is already accomplished there.

THE NATURAL (HERE) THE SPIRIT (THERE)

Here mortal men receive tithes, but there he receives them, of whom it is witnessed that he lives.

—Hebrews 7:8

As we see in Hebrews 7:8, the principle is present. "Here" mortal men receive tithes, and "there" He receives them...." Here represents the "natural," and the other represents the "spiritual." We live in the natural world, but there is also a spirit world. What we do here in the natural world has a profound impact on what happens in the spiritual realm. The dividing line between the two is the soul (mind, will, and emotions), and it is the area that can determine what will be experienced in the territories of either the natural or the spiritual.

Like Jesus, who was a life-giving Spirit brought forth by God's Word and the word of prophets and declarations throughout the Old Testament, the Body of Jesus took generations of the spoken word, ranging from God Almighty in Genesis, to the prophets, David in the Psalms, until finally the Word became flesh. Jesus is the Word made flesh *(see* John 1), and we must recognize these spiritual realities, or the living things in the realm of the spirit, come about in our lives in a similar way.

IF YOU WORK THE WORD, THE WORD WORKS

If you disrespect the godly principles of the Spirit, you'll get a disrespected manifestation in the natural. Sowing God's Word and principles and respecting the Spirit's godly principles will produce a supernatural reaction in the natural world. Whatever controls the territory of the mind will have a greater influence on a person's quality of life. Thoughts can alter the human experience and shape our beliefs.

> *For those who live according to the flesh set their minds on the things of the flesh, but those who live according to the Spirit, the things of the Spirit.* 6 *For to be carnally minded is death, but to be spiritually minded is life and peace.* 7 *Because the carnal mind is enmity against God; for it is not subject to the law of God, nor indeed can be.* 8 *So then, those who are in the flesh cannot please God.* 9 *But you are not in the flesh but in the Spirit, if indeed the Spirit of God dwells in you. Now if anyone does not have the Spirit of Christ, he is not His.* 10 *And if Christ is in you, the body is dead because of sin, but the Spirit is life because of righteousness.*
> 11 *But if the Spirit of Him who raised Jesus from the dead dwells in you, He who raised Christ from the dead will also give life to your mortal bodies through His Spirit who dwells in you.* 12 *Therefore, brethren, we are debtors—not to the flesh, to live according to the flesh.* 13 *For if you live according to the flesh you will die; but if by the Spirit you put to death the deeds of the body, you will live.* 14 *For as many as are led by the Spirit of God, these are sons of God.*
>
> —Romans 8:5-14

THE LAW OF THE MIND

> *For I delight in the law of God according to the inward man.* 23 *But I see another law in my members, warring against* ***the law of my mind****, and bringing me into captivity to the law of sin which is in my members.*
>
> —Romans 7:22-23

The mind is the veil that separates the natural and the spiritual. The law of the mind says you will receive and experience what you believe. For example, if you think God does not exist in the natural, you may receive some of what God promises by accident; however, you will not receive the things of the spirit. An unrenewed mind operates in the "flesh" or is "carnal." The flesh, or carnal mind, is simply a mind that relies solely on the five senses—what you see, hear, smell, taste, or feel. It has no relationship with the spiritual. The human mind is like an incubator of thought and meditation. What you meditate on long enough will be drawn into your natural experience. This is why taking every thought captive to the obedience of Christ is so vital. We must constantly challenge ourselves by asking: *What am I thinking about?* Whatever you are thinking and saying on a consistent and regular basis is what you will eventually experience.

THE NATURAL COMES FIRST

> *However, the spiritual is not first, but the natural, and afterward the spiritual.*
>
> —1 Corinthians 15:46

Notice the reference in 1 Corinthians 15:46 to the spiritual not being first—this is a remarkable statement. Most people would ask, "What is first, the spirit or the natural?" Often, many would respond by saying, "The spiritual." Why? Because they know this is the realm of God, they know that we should seek first the kingdom of God and His righteousness (*see* Matthew 6:33). Many scriptural truths would point us to believe that the realm of the spirit comes first in the order of things.

In context, this scripture speaks of the first Adam and the Last Adam. It explains that the first Adam was a natural man, and the Last Adam was a life-giving Spirit, straight from God. In this context, the principle is that *the spiritual is not first, but instead the natural is first.* Here is one principle you can take away from this scripture. There must be an action in the natural, which is faith, before a supernatural reaction can manifest from the spirit realm.

GETTING A SUPERNATURAL REACTION

An example would be *healing*. We know we are to lay hands on the sick and they will recover. This means there is a natural faith action of stretching out your physical hand and placing it on a person. A spiritual or supernatural reaction occurs with this biblical, natural action of faith. Healing will manifest in a physical body. Why doesn't it just happen straight from the Spirit? This is because the kingdom of God works through you—a natural, free, moral agent.

Similarly, salvation works through the natural preaching of the gospel. A preacher must open their mouth and release natural words by faith. Natural hearing occurs and a supernatural reaction happens when those who hear, believe and receive salvation in Jesus. That supernatural experience of salvation results from something that occurred first in the natural, which induced or permitted a supernatural encounter. A better way to understand this would be to say that humans are the gatekeepers to what is allowed into this natural world; ergo, first in the natural, then in the spiritual.

This graphic helps explain this topic. To experience a supernatural reaction, there must be a predicated natural action. This would be what we call a faith action. Faith actions often defy soulish logic and reason when the action takes you beyond the soulish barrier and accesses the realm of the spirit. Faith is like a bridge between the soul and the spirit, causing a supernatural reaction. Take prophecy, for example. When speaking out by faith in the natural word of the Lord, it bypasses the soulish veil into the realm of the spirit, causing a manifestation back into the natural. This is a simple picture of what I refer to as getting a supernatural reaction.[1]

> *And do not be conformed to this world, but be transformed by the* ***renewing of your mind****, that you may prove what is that good and acceptable and perfect will of God.*
>
> —Romans 12:2

Good teaching is the best form of deliverance. Because of a renewed mind to the Word of God, the devil cannot get to the believer directly.

THE SPIRIT REALM IS THE PARENT FORCE

When the mind is renewed, spiritual results in the natural will come. This natural world was not what birthed the spirit; the spirit realm birthed the natural realm. The spirit is the parent force; the greater the authority and creativity, the greater the reality. When believers renew their minds about what's done in the greater reality, it will manifest into the natural with horsepower that will break things free for them, and the devil won't be able to get at them.

An unrenewed mind is a carnal mind. One will reap in the realm of the spirit by ceasing to sow to the natural mind and renewing the mind to be fully persuaded that God's Word is truth.

GRACE AND FAITH

> *For by grace you have been saved through faith, and that not of yourselves; it is the gift of God,* [9] *not of works, lest anyone should boast.*
>
> —Ephesians 2:8-9

Renewing the mind doesn't automatically bring the blessing. Taking what's already been done in the spirit realm will draw it out. The Bible teaches us that we are saved by grace through faith.

Grace, by the Spirit, is God's part. Faith, in the natural, is our part. It's our cooperation and corresponding natural action to the spiritual. This is learned by renewing the mind to the Word of God.

An unrenewed, carnal mind is a mind that has no Word in it. Only memorizing the Word is not enough. It must get into the heart and change the thinking to be effective. The devil knows the Word better than almost anybody alive. He quoted scripture to Jesus, but Jesus was the Word made flesh; He had a renewed mind. He countered the devil's words by quoting scripture. "It is written…." (*see* Matthew 4:4-7 and Luke 4:4-10).

Victory in spiritual warfare begins when one is fully persuaded and transformed by renewing the mind. It's a mind that thinks the thoughts of the Lord, by reading the Bible until it starts talking back.

A WORD OF CAUTION

Some people will say, "All you need is God's grace. He loves you, and His grace will cover you." Others might say, "You don't need the Word of God—it's legalism—you're saved." While it is true that grace is abounding, it is harmful to think that the Word of God and renewing the mind to its truth are unnecessary. Don't fall for that lie. It is opening the door for the devil to move in with even more lies, so he can take over and bring destruction. What you don't know can hurt you.

When I feel like my spiritual battery is running low and needs a "jump-start," I go to Psalm 119, read it out loud in faith, connect my heart to His, and believe everything it says is for me. If you do that, I dare you to stay defeated. Exercising faith by putting yourself in those verses and speaking them aloud boldly will catapult you to a renewed mind.

THE DOMINO EFFECT

> *And Jesus answered and said to them: "Take heed that no one deceives*
> *you.* [8] *...All these are the beginning of sorrows.* [9] *Then they will deliver*
> *you up to tribulation and kill you, and you will be hated by all nations*
> *for My name's sake.* [10] *And then many will be offended, will betray one*
> *another, and will hate one another.* [11] *Then many false prophets will*
> *rise up and deceive many.* [12] *And because lawlessness will abound, the*
> *love of many will grow cold.* [13] *But he who endures to the end shall*
> *be saved."*
>
> —Matthew 24:4, 8-13

You are a free moral agent, capable of making your own decisions. You can choose right or wrong, believe truth or lies, serve or rebel, be free or in bondage. Free moral agents can be mighty weapons as sons and daughters of God or puppets of the devil. It's all based on your conviction in what you believe. Jesus tells us not to be deceived.

What I call the "domino effect" is one of the devil's best tools to attack your stance in Jesus. Let's say your mind is renewed to the Word of God, and you're standing firm in Christ Jesus. The devil is smart enough to know he cannot attack you directly because the Word will stop him. He knows he cannot touch you because you will make him pay. But the devil knows your schedule, he knows you pray, and he knows the same things about the people around you.

The devil uses the *domino effect* for his purposes. He will find someone to "help" get you off-kilter. The following example illustrates one way the devil can engage in spiritual warfare.

> ***Imagine waking up in the morning and starting your morning routine to get ready for the day. Everything starts just fine. The sun is shining, and the birds are singing. On the way to dropping your child off at school, you need to stop at your favorite gas station—it has the best prices. You insert your credit card, lift the handle, and push the button, but the pump doesn't start. You notice some pumps have bags over their handles, but others don't. You move to a different "unbagged" pump, and it's the same issue. You decide to go to another gas station, mildly frustrated, but you still have plenty of time to get gas.***
>
> ***The lines are long at the second, more expensive gas station. You realize they must be the spill-over from the first non-working station. Time is now running short. You hurry to the next station, even though it costs the most in your neighborhood, hoping you don't run out of gas before you get there. Now you're getting anxious and worried.***
>
> ***You are finally able to get gas. You say "Good morning" to the person at the next pump, but they are not in a good mood. They begin to yell about the high prices, the economy, and the world in general, and end with a curse about God. Worry and anxiety are getting stronger with the addition of anger. After all, all you did was say "Good morning!"***
>
> ***It's time to drop off your child at school. Someone in the drive-through line cuts you off and almost hits your car. They yell an obscenity at you, so you yell back, and now there is increased anger, further distress, and fear from a near collision.***
>
> ***Your next stop is at work. You arrive running late and don't have time for coffee. The boss wants to know why you're late, and at this point, you are emotionally charged and even think about***

> ***walking out. You've hit your threshold of what negativity you can handle in one morning.***
>
> ***This might be an exaggerated picture of an imaginary chaotic day, but it makes the point that sometimes what you face in your routine is not always a natural circumstance. Things that happen to cause anxiety or anger can be demonic. Please hear me; not everything that happens is a demonic scenario or a spiritual issue. Yet it does happen, and it comes subtly to throw you off from divine appointments.***

This scenario is what I call the domino effect, meaning demonic forces may not have direct access to you, so they attempt to affect those they can persuade. By influence, demonic forces can try to throw roadblocks in your path by messing with people to create frustration.

Because all of these people are free moral agents, they can experience a demonic influence working on their minds. They allowed the domino effect to shape their reactions, either through an unrenewed mind toward God's Word or their ignorance.

It's important to remember you may be experiencing the domino effect, not because you're doing something wrong, but because you're doing something right. If the devil can take your peace, he can get you to react carnally (from your five senses), which creates inroads into your soul (mind, will, and emotions).

That's why you need to be aware of his craftiness by being grounded in the Word of God. When you see spiritual warfare in the form of the domino effect rising in front of you, you can use the supernatural forces of joy, peace, righteousness, faith, and patience to punch right through the devil's schemes. There's no reason to give in to what you know that the Bible says you shouldn't give in to.

> *Be alert and of sober mind. Your enemy the devil prowls around like a roaring lion looking for someone to devour.*
>
> —1 Peter 5:8 NIV

> *Submit yourselves, then, to God. Resist the devil, and he will flee from you.*
>
> —James 4:7 NIV

I believe Jesus is awakening you. Your life may seem chaotic and even a little out of control, but Jesus Christ is the Voice of God. His Voice is roaring right now, like the Lion of Judah, and you can see victory over the domino effect by simply stepping toward Him through His written Word and prayer.

Remember, information brings peace. Data brings victory and helps you make good decisions. As a result, you don't have to surrender to the kingdom of darkness. God is calling you to step into a higher understanding of His calling.

> *But solid food belongs to those who are of full age, that is, those who by reason of use have their senses exercised to discern both good and evil.*
>
> —Hebrews 5:14

> *His divine power has given us everything we need for a godly life through our knowledge of Him who called us by His own glory and goodness.* [4] *Through these He has given us His very great and precious promises, so that through them you may participate in the divine nature, having escaped the corruption in the world caused by evil desires.*
>
> —2 Peter 1:3-4 NIV

There is a spirit world and a natural world. When we sow to the natural, we reap in the natural. When we sow to the spirit, we reap the things of the spirit. The mind is the gateway of renewal that directs us. That is why we need to renew our minds to the things of the spirit (*see* Romans 12:2). A mind renewed to the Word of God will bring spiritual results into the natural.

REJOICE THAT YOUR NAMES ARE WRITTEN IN HEAVEN

The bottom line on spiritual warfare is this:

> *Then the seventy returned with joy, saying, "Lord, even the demons are subject to us in your name."* [18] *And He said to them, "I saw Satan fall like lightning from heaven.* [19] *Behold, I give you authority to trample on serpents and scorpions, and over all the power of the enemy, and nothing*

> *shall by any means hurt you.* [20] *Nevertheless do not rejoice in this, that the spirits are subject to you, but rather rejoice because your names are written in heaven."*
>
> —Luke 10:17-20

Satan was allegedly the musician in heaven. Instead of worshiping, he wanted to be worshiped. He was arrogant and wanted to be like God. In doing so, he was cast out of heaven and fell like lightning to the earth.

This is the picture of spiritual warfare in heaven. The disciples rejoiced in being able to cast out demons in Jesus' name. Notice what Jesus told His disciples: Instead of rejoicing about being able to cast out demons, recognize that God has called and marked you. This is the joy by which we overcome the world—it's our faith. He said *you need* to *rejoice in your salvation. Be glad because your names are written in heaven, and as a by-product of your faith, demons have to submit to you.* Everything He has is already yours when your life is seated with Christ. See it from Jesus' perspective.

> *For everyone born of God overcomes the world. This is the victory that has overcome the world, even our faith.* [5] *Who is it that overcomes the world? Only the one who believes that Jesus is the Son of God.*
>
> —1 John 5:4-5 NIV

CHAPTER NINE

WEAPONS OF WAR

For though we walk in the flesh, we do not war according to the flesh. [4] For the weapons of our warfare are not carnal but mighty in God for pulling down strongholds, [5] casting down arguments and every high thing that exalts itself against the knowledge of God, bringing every thought into captivity to the obedience of Christ, [6] and being ready to punish all disobedience when your obedience is fulfilled.

—2 Corinthians 10:3-6

The flesh is a mindset, a way of thinking and functioning in line with the devil. Children of God do not walk in the flesh or war according to the flesh. Instead, believers use God's mighty weapons to pull down strongholds, bring every thought captive to the obedience of Christ (verse 5), and punish disobedience (verse 6). Obedience is impossible until the choice to renew the mind to the Word of God is made; the by-product is punishing disobedience. This means that the disobedient thought cannot come to fruition. If God asks His kids to do something, they will do it.

SOBER-MINDED EFFECTIVENESS

Faith must be applied to God's grace to renew the mind. Grace, given by God, is free. Faith is our part.

> *Therefore gird up the loins of your mind, be sober, and rest your hope fully upon the grace that is to be brought to you at the revelation of Jesus Christ.*
>
> —1 Peter 1:13

"Gird up the loins of your mind" originates from early biblical history, referring to the long robes men wore. If they tried running in a robe, they could trip and fall unless they "girded" themselves up. They would reach behind their ankles, pull the excess robe material from behind to the front, and tuck it into their belt. It now resembled a pair of trousers, and they could run unencumbered. The parallel to the mind is saying, Don't let the excess be there. Don't let any excess in your mind entangle your ability to move and think freely and lightly. In other words, discipline your thoughts to align with God's Word if you need to use your mental faculties to accomplish something.

First Peter 1:13 goes on to say, "Be sober." We are to rest our hope fully upon God's grace, which comes to us when we have a revelation of Jesus' finished work on the cross as it applies to us.

> *For I say, through the grace given to me, to everyone who is among you, not to think of himself more highly than he ought to think, but to think soberly, as God has dealt to each one a measure of faith.*
>
> —Romans 12:3

In Romans 12:3, Paul says, "Think soberly, and don't think of yourself as better than others." God has given everyone a measure of faith. Why is this important? Because these are places where the devil can access one's life. He can enter through pride, unforgiveness, or thoughts contradicting God's Word. Instead, we are to rest our hope entirely upon the grace brought to us at the revelation of Jesus Christ. Again, faith needs to be added to God's grace.

PEACE REPELLED SAUL'S DEMON

> *And so it was, whenever the spirit from God was upon Saul, that David would take a harp and play it with his hand. Then Saul would become refreshed and well, and the distressing spirit would depart from him.*
>
> —1 Samuel 16:23

To overcome the devil's powers, we must pivot our thoughts away from ourselves or what may be trying to bring torment, confront the devil with anointed music through praise and worship, and give God affection and attention.

In 1 Samuel 16, David played music for King Saul because demons tormented him. When David played the harp for Saul, the evil spirit would depart from him. There was no "in the name of Jesus" in the Old Testament, which shows that Jesus' name is not the only requirement. It also requires the cooperation of the person with the demonic influence. (I've tried to cast demons out of people who wanted to keep their demons, and they did.)

Saul had this demon repelled from him, but David didn't release the name of Jesus. What was it that repelled the demon? It wasn't the harp playing by itself; it was the anointed music of God on a man of God, David, that soothed the soul of Saul. His soul found peace, for a moment.

MUSIC BROUGHT PEACE TO ELISHA

Another example of the peace music can bring to an anxious soul is found in the story of the prophet Elisha in 2 Kings.

> *"But now bring me a musician." Then it happened, when the musician played, that the hand of the LORD came upon him.* [16] *And he said, "Thus says the LORD: 'make this valley full of ditches.'"*
>
> —2 Kings 3:15-16

The kings of Israel, Judah, and Edom approached Elisha to ask for help in defeating their common enemy, Moab. At first, Elisha was angry and told them to seek help from the prophets of their mothers and fathers because they walked in darkness. When Elisha realized that God had put the three kings together for His purpose, he knew seeking the Lord was vital, but his soul was in turmoil. Elisha was anxious and sought a musician to calm him. Once peace came into his soul, God could speak to him, and he could give the kings the word of the Lord.

When music soothed Saul's soul, he could make demons leave him. When the musician calmed Elisha's spirit, he could hear God's Voice. A demon cannot attack a soul in peace. Even unbelievers can drive away demons from their presence if they put their souls in order. This shows us that humans have more authority over the devil than we know.

As free moral agents, humans have a valve that can turn off or on the Spirit of God based on the peace in their souls, whether demonic spirits are attacking them or they are not at peace in their minds, just not for long.

YOU STILL NEED JESUS!

The demons may leave for the moment, but they will come back. People still need Jesus. Without being born again, you'll miss out on heaven, as well as all the promises God provides for you in this life through Jesus' death and resurrection. With Jesus, you get *super* on your *natural* and see a devastating effect on the kingdom of darkness.

As Jesus said, "Rejoice that your name is written in heaven" (*see* Luke 10:20). His salvation benefits include: you are saved, healed, delivered, preserved, protected, prosperous, and whole!

God needs you and His Church. He needs you to know who you are in Him and the authority He has given you. Remember, what you don't know can hurt you. It's time to go deep into the Word of God and wake up to your divine pursuit. Jesus is the Voice of God, and when you get the biblical revelation of spiritual warfare that works, you will rejoice that your name is written in heaven.

FULL METAL SOLDIER

> *Finally, my brethren, be strong in the Lord and in the power of His might.* [11] *Put on the whole armor of God, that you may be able to stand against the wiles of the devil.* [12] *For we do not wrestle against flesh and blood, but against principalities, against powers, against the rulers of the darkness of this age, against spiritual hosts of wickedness in the heavenly places.* [13] *Therefore take up the whole armor of God, that you may be able to withstand in the evil day, and having done all, to stand.*
>
> —Ephesians 6:10-13

The devil is working overtime, using his schemes (or wiles) to trick you. He uses nefarious plans to try to destroy your life. *Kakodaímon* is a Greek word that represents the devil and means *evil genius/spirit.* Satan is trying to get you to fall into his trap through persuasion. He's a roaring lion, and he's trying to snare you. However, we see in Psalm 91:3 that God shall "deliver you from the snare of the fowler." The fowler is the devil. Knowing the Word is critical in your fight against him!

We find out with whom and where the battle occurs in Ephesians 6:12: "For we do not wrestle against flesh and blood, but against *principalities*, against *powers*, against *the rulers of the darkness of this age*, against *spiritual hosts of wickedness* in the heavenly places." This is the essence of spiritual warfare. The battle is not with people or the natural things of this world, so we cannot fight with natural weapons. The battle is spiritual. We are in a war against principalities, powers, and rulers of this dark age—Satan and his demonic forces. However, God gives us spiritual weapons for victory! We must learn to utilize them. It's spiritual warfare that works.

TAKE UP THE WHOLE ARMOR AND STAND IN VICTORY

Ephesians 6:13 says, "Therefore take up the whole armor of God, that you may be able to withstand in the evil day, and having done all, to stand." "Having done all, to stand" refers to a military or arena fighting mindset. Gladiators in the arena at the time this was written had the mentality that they would overcome no matter what; they would stand and win.

Unfortunately, a popular religious teaching regarding "stand" in these verses does not hold up as truth in spiritual warfare. This teaching says, "You've given it your all. You've done all you can. You fought so hard and did everything, but it didn't work. You tried. You told God how hard you tried, but it was too hard."

This teaching is misleading. It allows people to indulge in self-pity, believing that pity will move God. Too many people believe that God is moved by their needs. If God moved by need, every impoverished nation, city, and person would flourish overnight. God is moved by *faith*. People must change their thinking and beliefs to align with God's Word. If you're in a difficult battle, know how much Jesus loves you. He loves you right now, no matter what you're going through, and it will be alright.

Ephesians 6:13 says, "...that you may be able to withstand in the evil day, and having done all, to *stand*." Don't believe the enemy's lies that may come to you through well-meaning people or unanointed religious teaching. These statements, for example, are false according to the Word of God. The following are examples that show what "stand" does *not* mean:

- I've tried everything, God. You must not want me to be successful.
- I've lost it all. I guess You didn't want me to have it, Lord.
- We did everything the doctors told us, but our baby died anyway. God must have needed another angel in heaven.
- I've attended church since I was a child. I always try to do good. Why is there so much chaos in my life?

Not true! To *stand* does not mean you've tried everything that didn't work—now, you're just going to stand there and get beaten up. "Stand" in Ephesians 6:11 speaks about *a contender.* The contender says, "I'm going into the battle with the knowledge I'm trained and prepared—I've done it all." It's not standing to endure. It's standing to get your reward, win, and receive your prize. The battle is not over until you win!

THE FULL ARMOR OF GOD

> *Stand firm then, with the belt of truth buckled around your waist, with the breastplate of righteousness in place,* [15] *and with your feet fitted with the readiness that comes from the gospel of peace.* [16] *In addition to all this, take up the shield of faith, with which you can extinguish all the flaming arrows of the evil one.* [17] *Take the helmet of salvation and the sword of the Spirit, which is the word of God.* [18] *And pray in the Spirit on all occasions with all kinds of prayers and requests. With this in mind, be alert and always keep on praying for all the Lord's people.*
>
> —Ephesians 6:14-18 NIV

The whole armor of God has everything to do with the Word of God in you. It's a practice and a discipline.

BELT OF TRUTH

Ephesians 6:14 says, "With the belt of truth buckled around your waist." "Buckled" is past tense, meaning *it's something you've already done by discipline.* Preparation has been put into practice, so you're always prepared.

The Roman centurion soldier wore a "belt" that held all the armor together. The belt of truth is daily Bible reading and studying. The Word of God established in the heart holds everything together in the life of a believer.

> *Sanctify them by Your truth. Your word is truth.*
>
> —John 17:17

BREASTPLATE OF RIGHTEOUSNESS

Next, put on the *breastplate of righteousness*. A born-again child of God is considered righteous—in right standing with God.

> *And Jesus increased in wisdom and stature, and in favor with God and men.*
>
> —Luke 2:52

Righteousness means you have a revelation of the finished work of Jesus and all He has done for you. As you increase in wisdom and stature, you'll grow in favor with God and man by behaving rightly toward your brothers and sisters.

FEET FITTED FOR THE GOSPEL

Ephesians 6:15 says, "And with your feet fitted with the readiness that comes from the gospel of peace." This refers to the complete gospel. You know that God loves you and that His promises are true. You have the Word deep inside and are ready to go in and out of season. This is preparatory living, and it is your lifestyle. You are prepared to take the gospel of peace into whatever situation.

SHIELD OF FAITH

Continuing to verse 16 (NIV), it says, "In addition to all this, take up the shield of faith, with which you can extinguish all the flaming arrows of the evil one." This verse switches from past tense, what is done in the past to prepare, to present tense. Verses 14 and 15 are the *logos* (written Word of God) preparation of the Word. It's your daily lifestyle, and you receive revelation from your studies. Verse 16 is the *rhema,* or spoken word. When the things the enemy tries to bring on you, like slander, theft, losses, or sickness, to infiltrate your mind and actions, you're ready. What you've put in your mind activates you for what is coming. In other words, you have so much Word in you that when the fiery darts of the wicked arise and try to assault you, you recognize the lie. The shield of faith stops that lie from taking root in you. It is extinguished.

HELMET OF SALVATION

Ephesians 6:17 says, "Take the helmet of salvation." This helmet of salvation is a mindset renewed to God's Word. Your salvation ensures you are saved, healed, delivered, preserved, protected, prosperous, and whole. You know no devil, darkness, or sickness can come near you because you are covered.

SWORD OF THE SPIRIT

In Ephesians 6:17, we are also told to take "the sword of the Spirit, which is the word of God." In Greek, *distomos* is *a double-edged sword or a sword with two mouths.*

> *For the Word of God is living and powerful, and sharper than any two-edged sword, piercing even to the division of soul and spirit, and of joints and marrow, and is a discerner of the thoughts and intents of the heart.*
>
> —Hebrews 4:12

God's Word, when spoken, is powerful. Your words can stop the enemy in his tracks. Jesus responded to the devil in the wilderness by speaking God's Word over each temptation (*see* Matthew 4:4-11 and Luke 4:3-12). The devil could not win against the Word.

Finally, Ephesians 6:18 (NIV) reminds us always to be watchful of the enemy's schemes and *to pray in the Spirit on all occasions with all kinds of prayers and requests. Be alert and always keep on praying for all the Lord's people.* These verses in Ephesians show us how to be winning combatants in spiritual warfare.

Many people have warfare going on in their lives. It could be supernatural manifestations, demonic encounters, depression of the mind, offense, sickness or disease, or anything else the devil tries to bring to attack them. Just know that God is bringing you life and liberty in every area of your life. He wants you to experience the joy of winning all spiritual battles. The

Lord loves you. He loved you from your first breath and wants you to know everything He has already provided for you. It's time for you to learn what He's already promised.

> *May God give you more and more grace and peace as you grow in your knowledge of God and Jesus our Lord.* [3] *By his divine power, God has given us everything we need for living a godly life. We have received all of this by coming to know him, the one who called us to himself by means of his marvelous glory and excellence.* [4] *And because of his glory and excellence, he has given us great and precious promises. These are the promises that enable you to share his divine nature and escape the world's corruption caused by human desires.*
>
> —2 Peter 1:2-4 NLT

SECTION THREE

NEW COVENANT HORSEPOWER

CHAPTER TEN

PRESERVATION OF JESUS' BLOODLINE

In previous chapters, we discussed the different arenas of spiritual warfare. The most crucial of these is the war for our minds. Once we know our power and authority in God's promises, His Word, and our true identity in Christ, we are equipped for the battle. The ultimate victory in spiritual warfare is a complete focus and attention on Jesus and His finished work.

The goal of the body of Christ is to win people to Jesus and usher in God's kingdom on earth. Attacks of the devil are designed to blind people so they don't find Jesus. When people can't "see" Jesus and their focus lands on the demonic kingdom of darkness, they have begun to lose the battle. That's why you need to understand spiritual warfare that works, so you are equipped to win the war.

WISDOM FROM JUDE

The Book of Jude helps pull back the veil and reveals more about celestial dignitaries, supernatural entities, demons, and angels. Jude offers an interesting narrative, although some things are controversial. Sometimes, the simple truth can be overanalyzed, even if things seem clear. There are many things we can learn that relate to spiritual warfare. There's a "leapfrog" narrative of comparison and contrast between people who will be judged and angelic stories.

> *But I want to remind you, though you once knew this, that the Lord, having saved the people out of the land of Egypt, afterward destroyed those who did not believe.*
>
> —Jude 1:5

God gives us an understanding of the parallels between the Israelites who did not enter the promised land and the destruction that is to come in the judgment of the ungodly. He then pulls back the curtain to give us a quick snapshot of something that happened in the celestial realms behind the scenes in verse 6:

> *And the angels who did not keep their proper domain, but left their own abode, He has reserved everlasting chains under darkness for the judgment of the great day.*
>
> —Jude 1:6

The angels did not keep their proper domain. They decided to leave the realm and place of authority where God had placed them. It would be like seeing a fish climb a tree, a bird living underwater, or a turtle flying. It doesn't make sense. Angels left what they were created for and rebelled against God, so "He has reserved everlasting chains under darkness for the judgment of the great day."

The angelic entities mentioned in verse 6, who were following the leadership of Lucifer, went down the wrong path, as shown in verse 7:

> *As Sodom and Gomorrah and the cities around them in a similar manner to these, having given themselves over to sexual immorality have gone after* ***strange flesh,*** *are set forth as an example, suffering the vengeance of eternal fire.*
>
> —Jude 1:7

The term "strange flesh" in verse 7 does not just refer to sexual immorality, though that was a part of it. The narrative of Sodom and Gomorrah in Genesis 19 occurred after the flood. In these verses, we see another instance of *strange flesh,* adding more meaning to the term.

> *Now the two angels came to Sodom in the evening, and Lot was sitting in the gate of Sodom. When Lot saw them, he rose to meet them, and he bowed himself with his face toward the ground. [2] And he said, "Here now, my lords, please turn in to your servant's house and spend the night, and wash your feet; then you may rise early and go on your way." And they said, "No, but we will spend the night in the open square." [3] But he insisted strongly; so they turned in to him and entered his house. Then he made them a feast, and baked unleavened bread, and they ate. [4] Now before they lay down, the men of the city, the men of Sodom, both old and young, all the people from every quarter, surrounded the house. [5] And they called to Lot and said to him, "Where are the men who came to you tonight? Bring them out to us that we may know them carnally."*
>
> —Genesis 19:1-5

Lot offered the men of the town his virgin daughters instead of the angels, but they didn't want the daughters. The men of the city wanted the angels because they knew there was something familiar about their flesh. When they went after "strange flesh," it shows these city men were demonized. This is a strange narrative, but it has threads of truth.

In Genesis 3:15, the immediate prophecy God gave the devil after the fall was: "And I will put enmity between you and the woman, and between your seed and her Seed; He shall bruise your head, and you shall bruise His heel." This was saying that Jesus the Redeemer was coming, and He would be born of a woman. This signified a bloodline. The ultimate spiritual warfare began at that moment. It was a weaponized plan to pollute the bloodline before Jesus could be born, so He wouldn't be able to be born. The angels left their proper domain and accessed the realm of the natural to keep this from happening.

> *Likewise also these dreamers defile the flesh, reject authority, and speak evil of dignitaries.*
>
> —Jude 1:8

Jude 1:8 talks about those who are rebellious and headed for judgment and are apostates—those who once believed in God but rejected Him doctrinally in their behavior and rebellion against Him.

> *Yet Michael the archangel, in contending with the devil, when he disputed about the body of Moses, dared not bring against him a reviling accusation, but said, "The Lord rebuke you!"* 10 *But these speak evil of whatever they do not know; and whatever they know naturally, like brute beasts, in these things they corrupt themselves.* 11 *Woe to them! For they have gone in the way of Cain, have run greedily in the error of Balaam for profit, and perished in the rebellion of Korah.* 12 *These are spots in your love feasts, while they feast with you without fear, serving only themselves. They are clouds without water, carried about by the winds; late autumn trees without fruit, twice dead, pulled up by the roots;* 13 *raging waves of the sea, foaming up their own shame;* ***wandering stars*** *for whom is reserved the blackness of darkness forever.*
>
> —Jude 1:9-13

In verse 9, the narrative pivots again to the angelic narrative, where we see the archangel Michael contending with the devil over the body of Moses. Then, it pivots back in contrast with the apostate and rebellious people in verses 10 through 13.

The label "wandering stars" could have two understandings. First, it could be about people who are supposed to have a voice in the Christian community, but they turned away from God and misled people against Him. Second, it could mean angels in rebellion or demons symbolically "wandering stars." Revelation talks about several stars that were taken from heaven and followed the devil, the angels that went with him. There is no conclusion here, but it leans more toward those who turned away and rebelled. In any event, whoever it refers to "is reserved the blackness of darkness forever."

> *Now Enoch, the seventh from Adam, prophesied about these men also, saying, "Behold, the Lord comes with ten thousands of His saints,* 15 *to execute judgment on all, to convict all who are ungodly among them of all their ungodly deeds which they have committed in an ungodly way, and of all the harsh things which ungodly sinners have spoken against Him."*
>
> —Jude 1:14-15

Jude 1:14-15 references the Book of Enoch. Although this book is not recognized as part of the biblical canon, it inspired the excerpt that the ungodly will be judged.

> *These are grumblers, complainers, walking according to their own lusts; and they mouth great swelling words, flattering people to gain advantage.* [17] *But you, beloved, remember the words which were spoken before by the apostles of our Lord Jesus Christ:* [18] *how they told you that there would be mockers in the last time who would walk according to their own ungodly lusts.*
>
> —Jude 1:16-18

We must not walk according to lust if we want to be victorious in spiritual warfare.

> *These are sensual persons, who cause divisions, not having the Spirit.*
>
> —Jude 1:19

> *But solid food belongs to those who are of full age, that is, those who by reason of use have their senses exercised to discern both good and evil.*
>
> —Hebrews 5:14

Their five senses lead those who walk according to the lust of their flesh and cause divisions because they don't have the Spirit. This lifestyle is in direct contrast to Hebrews 5:14, which clearly states that we must exercise discernment to distinguish between *good* and *evil* and discipline our senses, or risk disbelief in God, which leads to a destructive outcome. People can choose to walk away from God if they decide to, but we look at spiritual warfare fundamentals here.

The basis of spiritual warfare is mind renewal, and the key to victory is functioning in the fruit of the Spirit: love, joy, peace, patience, kindness, goodness, meekness, gentleness, and self-control (*see* Galatians 5:22-23). One of the signs of people allowing the kingdom of darkness to rule in them is that they are *grumblers and complainers walking according to their own lusts* (Jude 1:16).

THE PLAN TO POLLUTE JESUS' BLOODLINE

Have you ever read the Old Testament and wondered why God would wipe out every man, woman, child, and animal? Why did He kill them all? Isn't He the God of love and mercy? Yes, He is, but He had to do it for a reason.

God's fallen angels were of mixed blood, and that rendered them irredeemable. They could not be allowed to exist in the natural world. If He had not wiped them out, they would have polluted the bloodline, or lineage, of Jesus. Jesus was born from a spiritual, not natural, encounter that needed to result in a pure virgin birth. These verses from Genesis explain how the fallen angels tried to prevent that from happening.

> Now it came to pass, when men began to multiply on the face of the earth, and daughters were born to them, [2] that ***the sons of God*** saw the daughters of men, that they were beautiful; and they took wives for themselves of all whom they chose.
>
> —Genesis 6:1-2

The sons of God mentioned in verse two are the same reference as in Job 1, which says the sons of God presented themselves before the Lord. This is speaking of angels. The angels saw the daughters of men, thought they were beautiful, and took them as wives for themselves. This is where the Lord begins to pivot the narrative. He was not looking to destroy the whole world. Instead, in verse 3, He limits man's lifespan to 120 years.

> And the LORD said, "My Spirit shall not strive with man forever, for he is indeed flesh; yet his days shall be one hundred and twenty years."
>
> —Genesis 6:3

Why was this such a big deal? Satan and the fallen angels wanted to dominate spiritually in the natural world. When the angels procreated with women, they polluted the bloodline that would ultimately lead to Jesus. The children that these relationships created produced physical beings known as giants, as seen in verse 4.

> There were ***giants*** on the earth ***in those days, and also afterward,*** when the sons of God came in to the daughters of men and they bore children to them. Those were the mighty men who were of old, men of renown.
>
> —Genesis 6:4

"In those days, and also afterward," means there was no particular end to those days before and after the flood of Noah's time. They weren't all wiped away in the flood. Remember Goliath? He was around after the flood. We also see this in the narrative of Joshua and Caleb, who went into the Promised Land to scout it out. They saw there were giants in the land. Some people have speculated that these giants were nine to thirty feet tall. Indeed, some extra-biblical studies suggest they had several rows of sharpened teeth. The spies with Joshua and Caleb said they looked like grasshoppers to the giants (*see* Numbers 13:33).

BLOODLINE PRESERVATION THROUGH NOAH

God had prophesied that His Son was coming from the very beginning. The seed of the woman would destroy the devil, and he knew he had seasons of time, but no determined time. He had generations to plant minefields of bloodline pollution into the world.

> *But Noah found grace in the eyes of the LORD.* [9] *This is the genealogy of Noah. Noah was a just man,* **perfect in his generations.** *Noah walked with God.*
>
> —Genesis 6:8-9

Noah was a just man, found grace in the eyes of the Lord, and was "perfect in his generations." Noah was not a perfect guy. We see that after the flood, in the colorful story of his inappropriate behavior and the perversion with his family. Noah was drinking, fell, and passed out naked in his tent, and things happened with his sons. Noah wasn't exactly the poster child for good behavior. He wasn't perfect in a personhood sense. When verse 9 says, "This is the genealogy of Noah. Noah was a just man, perfect in his generations," it says he was perfect in his bloodline. His generations were pure. There was no demonic or angelic interference in his bloodline.

Because a pure bloodline was needed for Jesus to be born, God needed to wipe out the "strange flesh" giants in the Old Testament. It's why God had His people stand up, take territory, and seize cities to shut things down. Old Testament warriors battled with swords, shields, and other weaponry to kill these entities. That's a significant theme in the Old Testament. Therefore, when you see God judging cities, torching areas, and wiping whole populations off the map, it is because He was preserving Jesus' ability to be born for our sake.

In addition, there's a reason why when people died in the Old Testament, they went to "Abraham's bosom." People during this time had no Jesus or His blood to save them. Yet, God wanted to hold them for the time when Jesus would come on the scene. God was doing everything He could to keep, or hold back, what Adam lost. The devil was doing everything he could to thwart the plan of God. This explains why the violence, death, and craziness during the time of the Old Testament do not line up with the character of God we see in the New Testament. Everything has been transformed through Jesus. The weapons of our warfare against the spirit of darkness have changed. They no longer need to be carnal.

CHAPTER ELEVEN

JESUS CHANGES EVERYTHING

Four hundred years passed between the end of the Old Testament and the time of Jesus. Once we get to the New Testament, everything changes. In this chapter, you'll learn what dealing with demonic entities today means.

> *And I remind you of the angels who did not stay within the limits of authority God gave them but left the place where they belonged. God has kept them securely chained in prisons of darkness, waiting for the great day of judgment.*
>
> —Jude 1:6 NLT

ANGELS, FALLEN ANGELS, AND DEMONS

Jude 1:6 refers to the angels who did not remain in their appointed place, and as a result, God confined them to chains to await their judgment on a specific day. We must consider these fallen angels when engaging in spiritual warfare and casting out demons. Many think the demons we fight today are the angels mentioned in Jude 1:6. There's an argument for it, but I see something more. What if the demons we cast out are not those demons but something else?

> *Then the sixth angel sounded: And I heard a voice from the four horns of the golden altar which is before God,* 14 *saying to the sixth angel who*

> *had the trumpet, "Release the four angels who are bound at the great river Euphrates."* [15] *So the four angels, who had been prepared for the hour and day and month and year, were released to kill a third of mankind.* [16] *Now the number of the army of the horsemen was two hundred million; I heard the number of them.*
>
> —Revelation 9:13-16

The sixth angel is an angel of God, and it talks about the bottomless pit and its circumstances. Four angels are bound in the river Euphrates. This could refer to what's mentioned in Jude 1:6, which discusses the angels who left their proper abode and were bound by chains, awaiting the great day of judgment.

Many fallen angels were bound, but could it be that these fallen angels still do things on earth? We see in the Book of Daniel where His angels had to fight through (presumably) fallen angels. For example, the archangel Michael had to fight the prince of Persia to get a message to Daniel (*see* Daniel 10:13).

We also know Jesus cast these entities out because John 12:31 says, "Now is the judgment of this world; now the ruler of this world will be cast out." This includes the devil and all his authority in those realms.

OUR WAR IS AGAINST DISEMBODIED, FOUL, AND EVIL SPIRITS

Ultimately, what believers war against day-to-day is demons themselves. What is clear from the Bible is that we have the authority to drive out demons, and I want to present you with this: The demons we fight are not fallen angels. The Bible presents a compelling argument on this matter. I believe demons are disembodied, foul, and evil spirits.

Jesus said that when you cast out a demon, it goes into dry places looking for a place to rest (*see* Matthew 12:43). It's looking for another human body, a host to hijack. They feed on thoughts and actions to fulfill their evil desires through a physical body so they can do their duty in this world.

OLD TESTAMENT INTERACTION WITH DEMONS

In the Old Testament, the bodies that demons inhabited were killed. Therefore, they no longer had access to or authority in the natural world unless people gave in to their persuasion and let the demons influence them. The fiery darts of the enemy, mind control, and mind games allow demons to be empowered when people take them in.

When a demon tortured Saul, no one could make it leave except when Saul's soul found peace. David played the harp to soothe Saul's mind, and the demon departed. Jesus appears in the New Testament scene for the first time in scripture. He's the last Adam and has authority. Jesus' words drove out disembodied, parasitical demonic spirits living in a host's body. They obeyed Him.

ANGELS AND POSSESSION

Angels have a different role to play. Angels and demons are very different; angels rarely try to possess a person. But demons always try. The only thing I have to pivot on is when Satan, a fallen angel, entered Judas (*see* Luke 22:3; John 13:27). There is a consideration there. However, as the general theme, I see demons as disembodied spirits, not angels entering people.

REBUKE IS NOT A MAGIC WORD

> *When Jesus saw that the people came running together, he rebuked the foul spirit, saying unto him, Thou dumb and deaf spirit, I charge thee, come out of him, and enter no more into him.*
>
> —Mark 9:25 KJV

Jesus shows us how we are to deal with demons, and this is spiritual warfare that works.

In Mark 9:25, Jesus rebuked a foul spirit and told it to come out of the deaf and nonspeaking (dumb) boy. You often hear Christians using the phrase, "I rebuke you," when they see a demon manifesting in someone. "Rebuke" is not the magic word for casting out demons. "Rebuke" means *to express sharp disapproval or criticism about something*. Jesus defined the demonic spirit that was attacking the boy. In this instance, the foul spirit was the spirit of deafness and dumbness. Then, He gave it a direct reprimand and told it where it was to go. Saying, "I rebuke you," is ineffective in bringing the offender—in this case, the demon—to the conviction needed for it to leave.

Another example: In Matthew 8:26, Jesus commands the wind and waves to be still and rebukes them. Also in Mark 4:

> *And a great windstorm arose, and the waves beat into the boat, so that it was already filling.* [38] *But He was in the stern, asleep on a pillow. And they awoke Him and said to Him, "Teacher, do You not care that we are perishing?"* [39] *Then He arose and rebuked the wind, and said to the sea, "Peace, be still!" And the wind ceased and there was a great calm.* [40] *But He said to them, "Why are you so fearful? How is it that you have no faith?"*
>
> —Mark 4:37-40

Jesus spoke peace to the wind and waves, rebuking them. This was to counter the chaos and command peace to the situation. He wasn't rebuking the storm; He was rebuking the chaos causing the storm.

In the case of demons, we deal with them just like Jesus did because He gave us power over unclean spirits. Jesus made us the deciding factor in spiritual warfare. Jesus made a display of all these powers of darkness, principalities, angelic powers, and demons, and stripped them of their power. "Rebuke" is a word used for action.

USING THE WORD "REBUKE" IN SPIRITUAL WARFARE

Knowing how to use the word "rebuke" when dealing with spiritual warfare is essential. Identifying what needs to be rebuked is necessary. That's what Jesus did. He identified the spirit, and then He countered it with His words. Another definition of rebuke is *to counter and enforce the power of God with your words*. Is it a demon that needs to exit a person? In that case, you need to know what the demon is. For example, if someone needs healing:

- It is the spirit of sickness or infirmity, and you can name the sickness: flu, cold, cancer, etc.

- Emotionally or mentally troubled, it could be the spirit of mind control, chaos, or confusion.

When you pray for the sick, you're abusing that demon by enforcing the covenant of healing that Jesus' stripes provided for us. Whatever the demonic activity is, you are telling it to go.

The wind and sea were in chaos, and trained fishermen were terrified. They knew how to read the sky and were skilled in the sea. The storm came on suddenly. I believe the storm was demonic and was trying to kill them, and this is why Jesus rebuked it by saying, "Peace, be still," which released peace over it. He was speaking to the spirits working behind that natural phenomenon.

THE "REAL" KINGDOM OF DARKNESS

Many fear the kingdom of darkness and the devil. The devil is like the great Oz behind the curtain, trying to manipulate through mind control but without any power to back it up. Demons can only exert their influence if people surrender to them. That's why witchcraft is such a joke to people who are fire-baptized, filled with the Holy Spirit, and know the name of Jesus and all His name stands for. They know who they are in Christ, the Word abides in them, and they abide in the Lord.

However, to believers who do not know their identity in Christ, witchcraft is scary. Free moral agents have empowered demons. But just like in *The Wizard of Oz*, we would not be so scared if we pulled back the curtain to see what they looked like. I've had visions of demonic entities. Sometimes they're little, sometimes they're big. They often resemble small, furry creatures with large mouths that speak loudly. They're boisterous and experts at influencing your mind to go in their direction. When you give in to them, they become empowered.

> *Those who see you will gaze at you, and consider you, saying: "Is this the man who made the earth tremble, who shook kingdoms?"*
>
> —Isaiah 14:16

All the people in all the nations are going to see Satan, or Lucifer, for who he is. The reaction will be: "Really? I thought he was mighty. I thought he was huge, ugly, and fierce-looking." He's not, but the problem is that he is skilled at his craft and an expert at influencing people's minds and thoughts. Therefore, the nations can be deceived by him, and that's why the world is going into chaos.

But through Jesus, we have power and authority, the fruit of the Spirit, and the whole armor of God, which is how we defeat the powers of darkness.

> *Therefore, since we have this ministry, as we have received mercy, we do*
> *not lose heart.* [2] *But we have renounced the hidden things of shame, not*
> *walking in craftiness nor handling the word of God deceitfully, but by*
> *manifestation of the truth commending ourselves to every man's conscience*
> *in the sight of God.* [3] *But even if our gospel is veiled, it is veiled to those*
> *who are perishing,* [4] *whose minds the god of this age has blinded, who do*
> *not believe, lest the light of the gospel of the glory of Christ, who is the*
> *image of God, should shine on them.* [5] *For we do not preach ourselves, but*
> *Christ Jesus the Lord, and ourselves your bondservants for Jesus' sake.* [6]
> *For it is the God who commanded light to shine out of darkness, who has*
> *shone in our hearts to give the light of the knowledge of the glory of God*
> *in the face of Jesus Christ.*
>
> —2 Corinthians 4:1-6

The devil, the god (little "g") of this world, the prince of this age, has blinded the minds of this culture and the generations of this world through deception. Look at this progression: Satan's ultimate deception is to get people away from God, keep them from knowing who they are in Christ, and keep them from believing His promises. However, if they completely believe the promises and realize who they are in Christ, then the devil will try to persecute them for the sake of the Word.

PERSECUTION FOR THE WORD'S SAKE

> *And lest I should be exalted above measure by the abundance of the revelations, a thorn in the flesh was given to me, a messenger of Satan to buffet me, lest I be exalted above measure.*
>
> —2 Corinthians 12:7

The devil stirs up persecution, as we see in Paul's account of the "thorn in his flesh." Spiritual warfare is persecution, mind games, not believing everything that God has for you, using people against you, or becoming prideful. It's all designed to slow you down and ultimately hinder your effectiveness for the kingdom of God. His main approach is to deceive and blind people's minds so they don't believe God exists, and they do not want to find out who Jesus is. If you do, he tries to keep you from receiving what is yours as a believer.

PREACH THE GOSPEL FOR THE WIN!

We fight these "blinded minds" by preaching and demonstrating God's power to them.

> *But rise and stand on your feet; for I have appeared to you for this purpose, to make you a minister and a witness both of the things which you have seen and of the things which I will yet reveal to you.*
>
> —Acts 26:16

Being a minister and witness of the Lord Jesus Christ is one way we fight against the devil's evil scenario. How do we do this? Praying for unbelievers or those who are misinformed is a form of spiritual warfare. There is a specific way to pray for them to engage God and His armies at a high level.

> *Then Jesus went about all the cities and villages, teaching in their synagogues, preaching the gospel of the kingdom, and healing every sickness and every disease among the people.* [36] *But when He saw the multitudes, He was moved with compassion for them, because they were weary and scattered, like sheep having no shepherd.*
>
> —Matthew 9:35-36

Jesus recognized the state of the people He encountered. As His followers, we must have compassion for unbelievers and reach out to them. Evangelize because they're scattered like sheep without a shepherd. They don't know God.

> *Then He said to His disciples, "The harvest truly is plentiful, but the laborers are few.* [38] *Therefore pray the Lord of the harvest to send out laborers into His harvest."*
>
> —Matthew 9:37-38

Matthew 9:37-38 is a prayer of spiritual warfare. Jesus was moved by those who were scattered like sheep without a shepherd. They were lost, wandering aimlessly, unsure of who God was. They had not found who or what they were looking for. It's the song of the unbeliever asking, "Where is the answer?" Many are not hearing the truth right now.

USING PRAYER IN SPIRITUAL WARFARE

That is why this spiritual warfare prayer in Matthew 9:37-38 is powerful. To those who pray in Jesus' name, *pray to the Lord of the harvest that He would send His laborers into His harvest.* God cannot just make people get born again by you praying, "Save them, God," and suddenly they're saved and walking with the Lord. Minds don't automatically change as a result of that type of prayer. There has to be a confrontation with the truth and a decision to be made.

> *How then shall they call on Him in whom they have not believed? And how shall they believe in Him of whom they have not heard? And how shall they hear without a preacher?*
>
> —Romans 10:14

How will they hear without a preacher? How will they hear without one being sent? God has to engage them. An example is the story of Saul, who later became Paul, on the road to Damascus, found in Acts 9. He was going forward on the road and had an encounter with Jesus that changed his life. I think the saints' prayers were heard and manifested over time. Saul was persecuting the Jews, and I believe they must have prayed to God for help to empower them to stand against and not fear Saul's threats and abuse.

Saul thought he was doing the right thing, but Jesus appeared, knocked him to the ground, put scales on his eyes to blind him, and sent him to "Straight Street" to await further instructions. Saul had an unforgettable encounter with the Lord Jesus, but he needed an education in the truth of the Word to be completely transformed. God sent Ananias, anointed to be a laborer "into His harvest," to give Saul the gospel. It wasn't until Ananias broke it down for him that the scales fell off his eyes, and he became a disciple of Jesus (*see* Acts 9:10-19).

PRAY THE LORD OF THE HARVEST

Therefore pray the Lord of the harvest to send out laborers into His harvest.
—Matthew 9:38

> *Then He said to them, "The harvest truly is great, but the laborers are few; therefore pray the Lord of the harvest to send out laborers into His harvest."*
>
> —Luke 10:2

Real spiritual warfare is when you pray to the Lord of the harvest, and He begins to engage. Therefore, we *pray the Lord of the harvest to send out laborers into this harvest.* One way we pray this is by saying, "Remove the veil of blindness" from this person. When the veil is removed, someone can find the Lord.

The veil is pierced through the preaching of the gospel. Some harvesters are studying the Word, who know God and obey Him. God can raise, engage, and activate them to reach the person you're praying for. That's how we pray for the lost, for the unbelievers. We come into an agreement and say, "God, send laborers in their path," and God will do it.

THE LANDING PAD

God has given us power and authority over all the power of the enemy. To enforce what He has given us, we stand in absolute confidence in the name of Jesus and who we are in Christ. Demons know whether you believe or not. If people cast out the spirit of poverty like they cast out demons, they'd start to see good things happen in their finances. The same principle applies to sickness. You will see a breakthrough if you take your authority over anything given to you through Jesus' death and resurrection. This is the place we need to land on in spiritual warfare.

GOING RED IN THE BLOOD OF THE LAMB

Then I heard a loud voice saying in heaven, "Now salvation, and strength, and the kingdom of our God, and the power of His Christ have come, for the accuser of our brethren, who accused them before our God day and night, has been cast down. [11] And they overcame him by the blood of the Lamb and by the word of their testimony, and they did not love their lives to the death."

—Revelation 12:10-11

Revelation 12:10-11 discusses believers, specifically end-time saints. We recognize that the way to overcome the evil one is by the unpolluted bloodline of the Lamb, which has cleansed us and made us righteous. In addition, it says *we overcome by the word of our testimony*, which is our proven belief, track record, and tenure as a believer in Jesus. The bonus is not loving our life even unto death. If you want to win in spiritual warfare, Jesus said whoever tries to gain his life will lose it.

When you become a total disciple of Jesus, you no longer love your natural life.

The thief does not come except to steal, and to kill, and to destroy. I have come that they may have life, and that they may have it more abundantly.

—John 10:10

The exchange here is gaining a God-quality of life. "Life and life more abundantly" is yours. I encourage you to strengthen yourself and to "build yourself up in your most holy faith, praying in the Holy Spirit" (*see* Jude 1:20). Praying in the Spirit is a supernatural weapon that will cause you to stand.

You also stand firmly on Revelation 12:11. You overcome *by the blood of the lamb and the word of your testimony.* It's time to build yourself up. It's time to be strong in Jesus. It's time to know what He's done for you and the extreme extent God went to keep Jesus' bloodline pure. It was all necessary for it to reach you, as Jesus gave us the authority to drive out demons.

We even have authority at the end of the age, when celestial angels begin to collide and shake nations. As we remain in Him and His Word remains in us, we will see victory in this life like never before. Now is your time to rise against anything coming against you, whatever you're fighting.

CHAPTER TWELVE

THE GREAT COMMISSION

Later He appeared to the eleven as they sat at the table; and He rebuked their unbelief and hardness of heart, because they did not believe those who had seen Him after He had risen. [15] *And He said to them, "Go into all the world and preach the gospel to every creature.* [16] *He who believes and is baptized will be saved; but he who does not believe will be condemned.* [17] *And these signs will follow those who believe: In My name they will cast out demons; they will speak with new tongues;* [18] *they will take up serpents; and if they drink anything deadly, it will by no means hurt them; they will lay hands on the sick, and they will recover."*

—Mark 16:14-18

In Mark 16:14, Jesus was irritated with His disciples because their unbelief hardened their souls. Therefore, they could not be effective against the prince of the power of the air, who was defeated and cast out. He rebuked His disciples' unbelief because it gave the devil leverage, and He didn't want the devil to get a leg up on them.

We must believe in God's miracles and preach the Word of God. Creation itself responds to the gospel, the preaching of the good news. The highest form of spiritual warfare is when you preach the gospel. Mark 16:16 says, "He who believes and is baptized will be saved; but he who does not believe will be condemned." That's pretty clear, but it's not enough to be saved. You also have to renew your mind.

> *God is Spirit, and those who worship Him must worship in spirit and truth.*
>
> —John 4:24

> *It is the Spirit who gives life; the flesh profits nothing. The words that I speak to you are spirit, and they are life.*
>
> —John 6:63

In these verses in John, as far as Jesus Christ is concerned, *God is a Spirit, and those who worship Him must do so in spirit and truth.* Recognize this: The natural is the servant to the Spirit—the Word of God.

Mark 16:17 says that signs will follow those who believe, those whose natural persuasion is overtaken by the Spirit. Their thoughts, will, and emotions (their souls) are fully persuaded that Jesus Christ is Lord, and they significantly impact the natural.

> *I say then: Walk in the Spirit, and you shall not fulfill the lust of the flesh.*
>
> —Galatians 5:16

CASTING OUT DEMONS

As you renew your mind to the Word and believe what it says in Mark 16:17, you'll preach the gospel to every living creature and then have signs follow you. You'll cast out demons. Casting out demons is not necessarily a demonstrative display, like in the movies, where demons dramatically come out of someone. Sometimes, casting out demons comes through the power of persuasion, where you pray to change a mindset. If you are a believer, you should cast out demons in their areas of influence through preaching and/or changing people's mindsets.

For example, someone gives their life to Jesus, and suddenly, those demons are cast out—and you didn't even know it! It's because the person went from darkness to light; their mindset changed, and the demons had to let go. Sometimes, the demons come out with a shriek, or they're flamboyant, loud, disruptive, or just leave. But first and foremost, preach the gospel.

In addition to casting out demons, believers will speak with new tongues. Then it says they can take up serpents. However, as mentioned previously, that doesn't mean you can reach into a bucket in church and pull out snakes. That's not what this is talking about. It's about Paul's experience on the island of Malta (*see* Acts 28:1-10).

IT WILL BY NO MEANS HURT YOU

When Paul was shipwrecked on the island, he made a fire, and a snake latched onto his arm. What did he do? He shook it off into the fire and kept working. It will not harm you if you come in contact with anything dangerous, whether serpents or anything else.

I had an experience where a Rottweiler dog came at me, and it was almost demonic. This dog came running from a distance, and when it got close, it leaped to attack me. I took authority over it in Jesus' name, and the dog dropped to the ground, began running in circles around me, and finally ran away. That dog was not coming to check me out, but it could not attack and bite me. You can have authority over these kinds of animals, snakes, and scorpions because Mark 16:18 says, "They will take up serpents; and if they drink anything deadly, it will by no means hurt them; they will lay hands on the sick, and they will recover."

All of this is "The Great Commission." Unfortunately, many people discuss this topic but overlook the horsepower aspect. When we preach the gospel, we're supposed to be filled with power to drive out demons, speak in tongues, pick up serpents, and drink anything deadly, and it cannot hurt us. It means your body will have a supernatural, sustaining power. You will lay hands on the sick, and they shall recover because your body has supernatural health. This is the great commission and the highest form of spiritual warfare. People who preach the gospel have their minds renewed, and they go forward in power.

The formula is: Renew your mind to the Word of God, preach the gospel, and as a by-product, you will drive out demons, speak in tongues, and be protected from deadly or poisonous things. You can pray for the sick, and they will recover.

TAKING BACK DOMINION

He who sins is of the devil, for the devil has sinned from the beginning. For this purpose the Son of God was manifested, that He might destroy the works of the devil.

—1 John 3:8

Love has been perfected among us in this: that we may have boldness in the day of judgment; because as He is, so are we in this world.

—1 John 4:17

There is even more. God has called people to a high level. Why? Because God wants us to practice functioning in authority for the age to come. This world is not all there is to your experience. Whether your life is good, bad, or difficult, you have great hope because this is not all there is.

One of the many reasons God wants to fulfill the Great Commission is so He can teach us to take dominion. It's no different from the children of Israel who fought in the battle of Jericho, took back the land of Canaan, and drove out the giants and evil powers of that age. They took back what belonged to them. They won the physical battle. In our age, through Jesus, we win the spiritual battle.

PRACTICE FOR THE AGE TO COME

Then I saw a great white throne and Him who sat on it, from whose face the earth and the heaven fled away. And there was found no place for them.

—Revelation 20:11

Now I saw a new heaven and a new earth, for the first heaven and the first earth had passed away. Also there was no more sea.

—Revelation 21:1

Preaching the gospel is our job to drive out the remnants of evil. We enforce the kingdom now because it's practice for the age to come. Jesus is getting us ready for eternity. This is evident in Revelation 20:11 and Revelation 21:1.

Heaven and earth are going to go away from His face. We will not live in heaven forever. Heaven, as it is now, is going to flee away. Why is that? Because heaven has a stain of rebellion on it from the devil. It's been polluted. We must begin to take authority here, because we'll receive a new earth. We're practicing dominion and strength for the things in the coming age, but we won't dominate society by militarized control or taking over and commanding people. Many have tried to legislate Christianity in the past, and it didn't work well in the long run.

We're not here to legislate Christianity or to start a natural kingdom like the zealots wanted to do with Jesus. Instead, we're called to enforce the spiritual side through a natural manifestation. When we preach the gospel, we win hearts and minds through influence. Spiritual warfare turns into influence in the government, church, marketplace, entertainment, and every sector of society. But it's not us taking over those sectors. It's us influencing the hearts and minds of people until we cause influence in places of authority in those positions. This is how we bring cultural change, not through domination but influence.

HELL IS NOT ENOUGH FOR THE DEVIL

Once again, we are practicing for the time when heaven and earth pass away (*see* Revelation 21:1). There will be a new heaven and a new earth. God must recreate heaven because of Lucifer's sin. Consequently, this is also why hell is forever. Hell is not enough.

The punishment of hell is not enough to fit the crime that was committed against God. First, you need to understand the severity of the crime. Our finite minds cannot understand the level of holiness and perfection that is God. The best way to understand this is to balance God's perfection by looking at the severity of hell. Lucifer's crime is the antithesis to God's holiness. The devil lifted himself in pride and, with his angels, rebelled against God. He violated God's supernatural, perfect holiness. It was not a natural violation; it was an extreme spiritual violation.

The devil and his angels' transgression was so extreme that I believe hell was instantly created. Matthew 25:41 says hell was prepared for the devil and his angels. "Then He will also say to those on the left hand, 'Depart from Me, you cursed, into the everlasting fire prepared for the devil and his angels.'" Every action has a reaction. Hell burns forever because it cannot be enough to atone for the crime against God's holiness. However, there will be a day when hell comes to an end. It has a timeline, and at a certain point, it will be scooped up with all its inhabitants and cast into the *lake of fire*. That's called the second death (*see* Revelation 20:14).

WE ARE TERRESTRIAL BEINGS

> *There are also celestial bodies and terrestrial bodies; but the glory of the celestial is one, and the glory of the terrestrial is another.*
>
> —1 Corinthians 15:40

As human beings, we were not made to live in heaven forever. Heaven is a temporary solution because we were created to be terrestrial beings. If you were to die and leave this earth today, you would cross the veil, go into the realm of the spirit, and immediately be with the Lord (*see* 2 Corinthians 5:8). Jesus is the firstborn among many brethren (*see* Romans 8:29). He has a physical body and is seated in heaven. However, in the next age, He will rule for 1,000 years in His physical body on earth.

To prepare for Jesus' 1,000-year reign, we engage in spiritual warfare during our lives on earth, so we are ready to enforce the kingdom of God when we rule as kings and lords with Jesus. He is the King of kings and Lord of lords (*see* Revelation 19:16). We, as believers, are the kings and lords who will rule with Him in varying degrees of authority.

Practicing spiritual warfare by renewing minds, driving out demons, and taking territory by preaching the gospel is a proving ground for the authority we will have after this age. There is no gaining additional authority once we are in the age to come. Only what we do in this life will count in the next life.

We're going back to God's original design for the earth. The Garden of Eden was supposed to expand, but the devil's theft destroyed the original plan. We are here to expand it today. We will pick up where humanity left off in Genesis 1 in the coming age. In the meantime, we're advancing God's kingdom until the age to come arrives.

WE HAVE NEW TESTAMENT POWER!

One man of you shall chase a thousand, for the LORD your God is He who fights for you, as He promised you.

—Joshua 23:10

Joshua 23:10 describes how one man can overcome a thousand when God's presence and power come upon him. This is powerful! People in the Old Testament didn't yet have the New Covenant. Job is the oldest book in the Bible, and no covenant promises had been made that he could stand on during his time. He couldn't run the devil off.

However, the Word had been developed with Moses, as seen in Joshua 23. Joshua had been with Moses, and Joshua knew God differently from how Job knew Him. He knew one man could rout a thousand because he knew the covenant. The word "rout" means they could persecute and harass their enemies in close-quarters fighting. God anointed them for fighting, and He would fight for them.

Joshua, Samson, Elijah, and other Old Testament men could take territory because of God's covenant with Moses. When the anointing and Spirit of God came upon them, it didn't matter if they were strong in the natural. Their appearance and strength would not matter because God's supernatural power would come upon them, and they could rout a thousand. Isaiah 53:1 refers to "the arm of the Lord." The fleshly arm of people is not where their strength comes from. The "arm" of God represents His supernatural power and authority coming upon them to defeat their enemies.

In the Old Testament, the devil could do whatever he wanted. But now, in the New Testament, God's people have power over demonic entities. We have the authority to bind their power and change regions and people's lives by preaching the gospel. That's spiritual warfare.

You are of God, little children, and have overcome them, because He who is in you is greater than he who is in the world.

—1 John 4:4

Think about this: the weakest believer has more power in their little finger than all the powers of hell combined. Even though that's true, it does not scare the devil. He's not scared because you have more power or because Jesus lives inside you. What scares him is that one day, you will have a revelation of the *authority* you have in you. When you become a disciple-making machine and your mind is renewed to the Word of God, you become a clear-eyed and clear-minded weapon.

Show me a man or a woman of God who has their mind, will, and emotions (soul) surrendered to Jesus Christ, who is a disciple of the Word, who is not led by their emotions, and I'll show you someone who terrorizes the kingdom of darkness. These are the believers the devil is terrified of, and he will do everything he can to discredit them, lie about them, and persecute them. The devil wants to uproot the Word in you because it makes you a potent, terrorizing force to the kingdom of darkness.

This is true of mature believers who mix their faith with the words of Jesus. A mature believer exercises their senses to discern good and evil. They don't fluctuate. They stand with the Word, and it bears fruit for them. Spiritual warfare becomes effective when an experienced believer understands and puts it into practice.

SECTION 4

PRAYERS THAT PUNISH THE DARKNESS

CHAPTER THIRTEEN

WARFARE PRAYERS THAT PUNISH DARK POWERS

FUNDAMENTALS OF PRAYER

Therefore I exhort first of all that supplications, prayers, intercessions, and giving of thanks be made for all men.

—1 Timothy 2:1

Let's look at 1 Timothy 2:1. *Four types of prayer* are listed. There are more types of prayers throughout the Word of God, but this is a good foundation to begin with. Let's examine these four fundamental types of prayer, as each is closely tied to the Word of God.

FOUR TYPES OF PRAYER

1. SUPPLICATIONS

The Greek word here is *deesis*, meaning a *seeking, asking, entreating, or entreaty to God or man.*

And whatever you ask in My name, that I will do, that the Father may be glorified in the Son. [14] *If you ask anything in My name, I will do it.*

—John 14:13-14

> *Praying always with all prayer and supplication in the Spirit, being watchful to this end with all perseverance and supplication for all the saints.*
>
> —Ephesians 6:18

Paul prayed often for the churches, which is an entreating type of prayer. Jesus asked God for His people to be one with Him as He and the Father were one. This type of prayer is a request made just like the woman and the unjust judge (*see* Luke 18:1-8). It is asking and going to the Lord for a request.

2. PRAYERS

The Greek word used here is *proseuche*, meaning *a prayer of gathering*, which conveys the sense of praying together with others anywhere. Prayers from a united people caused Peter's miraculous release from prison. Acts 12:5 says Peter "was therefore kept in prison, but constant prayer was offered to God for him by the church." These together were very effective. This is the type of prayer at work in the story of an angel letting Peter out of prison. This story is humorous as it speaks to the unexpectedness of answered prayer.

> *And as Peter knocked at the door of the gate, a girl named Rhoda came to answer.* [14] *When she recognized Peter's voice, because of her gladness she did not open the gate, but ran in and announced that Peter stood before the gate.* [15] *But they said to her, "You are beside yourself!" Yet she kept insisting that it was so. So they said, "It is his angel."* [16] *Now Peter continued knocking; and when they opened the door and saw him, they were astonished.*
>
> —Acts 12:13-16

Here we see that the young girl, Rhoda, recognized Peter's voice and ran away excitedly to tell everyone in the house that Peter was there, leaving Peter outside. If we read between the lines just a little bit, she was saying, "Our prayers have been answered! Peter is at the door!" Here is the amusing part—they were all praying over the church, and according to Acts 12:5, they were also praying for Peter, who was in prison.

> *Peter was therefore kept in prison, but constant prayer was offered to God for him by the church.*
>
> —Acts 12:5

Scripture tells us how the group responded to her. They might as well have told her, "Don't interrupt us that Peter is released from prison! That's impossible, and that's why we are praying about this very thing right now!" Or, "Don't interrupt our praying session with a miracle answer! That's not possible!" The whole incident must have made God smile. Peter didn't even know he was awake when the angel took him out of the prison, and then when he got to the house, Rhoda ran away. The people praying for his release didn't believe what they were praying for could happen, so Peter had to keep pounding on the door to get noticed!

The point can be made that when you enact prayers of agreement with others, miraculous things begin to happen, even if you don't believe it when you see it!

I recall praying with a group of friends many years ago. It was over a dear friend caught up in an ungodly scenario. Instead of gossiping about this person or talking about the issue, we decided to come together in agreement. We held hands in a circle, about five or six of us, and we began to agree that this person's issue would be turned around. The problem was extreme, and there was little hope that we would ever see this person again. The very next day, everything changed. A complete reversal of heart, a change of direction, and a phone call said they released everything involving what they were entangled in. I know it was the result of the prayer of agreement. It was miraculous. Upon hearing the good news, it was similar to Rhoda telling the group, "Peter is at the door!"

When you find a group to agree with, don't be surprised when the impossible happens!

3. INTERCESSIONS

The Greek word used here is *enteuxis* prayer, which is addressing God for oneself or another.

Today, Jesus is our Great High Priest and intercessor. Yet we can hammer on something through prayer until it gives up or breaks through. Intercession is an entirely different prayer gear as we can agree and make requests. There is a mighty aspect of pushing through with this kind of prayer, which goes beyond a simple request or prayer of agreement. Intercession often involves a conflict that must be confronted in the spirit realm.

Jesus intercedes for you and me 24/7, while seated at the Father's right hand. No one can intercede like Jesus! What is He praying about regarding His people? Let's look at what Scripture says about this topic. We know that in the Book of Job, Satan was able to come before the throne of God with the sons of God, or the angels. However, something extraordinary has happened since that time.

First, we know that Satan was operating in Adam's authority to walk with God in the cool of the day. In other words, he possessed Adam's jurisdiction rights because Eve and Adam gave those to the devil. This, of course, is why the devil was able to tempt Jesus with all the kingdoms of the Earth. Dominion of the Earth's kingdoms had been given to him by Adam.

Since then, a great deal has changed. Let's recall when Satan wanted to sift Job, and the Lord said, "See, all he has is in your hand." Again, this was due to Adam giving up his seat of authority. Adam's authority is why the devil had access to destroy Job's life. God could only vouch for Job's life, but if Job could withstand the attacks, he would be justified in the end.

A similar event happened in Peter's life.

> *And the Lord said, **"Simon, Simon! Indeed, Satan has asked for you, that he may sift you as wheat.** 32 **But I have prayed for you,** that your faith should not fail; and when you have returned to Me, strengthen your brethren."*
>
> —Luke 22:31-32

Jesus prayed for Peter so that his faith would not fail. Uniquely, this was an intertestamental period. Jesus could pray for Peter, but Satan still had the jurisdiction to request to sift Peter.

> *Then I heard a loud voice saying in heaven, "Now salvation, and strength, and the kingdom of our God, and the power of His Christ have come, for the accuser of our brethren, who accused them before our God day and night, has been cast down."*
>
> —Revelation 12:10

This moment likely occurred when Jesus rose from the dead and took His rightful place, seated by the Father.

> *I will no longer talk much with you, for the ruler of this world is coming, and he has nothing in Me.*
>
> —John 14:30

> *Now is the judgment of this world; now the ruler of this world will be cast out.*
>
> —John 12:31

> *Who is he who condemns? It is Christ who died, and furthermore is also risen, who is even at the right hand of God,* ***who also makes intercession for us.***
>
> —Romans 8:34

> *For Christ has not entered the holy places made with hands, which are copies of the true, but into heaven itself,* ***now to appear in the presence of God for us.***
>
> —Hebrews 9:24

> *Therefore He is also able to save to the uttermost those who come to God through Him, since* ***He always lives to make intercession for them.***
>
> —Hebrews 7:25

> *For we do not have a High Priest who cannot sympathize with our weaknesses, but was in all points tempted as we are, yet without sin.*
>
> —Hebrews 4:15

WHEN THE ACCUSER COMES TODAY, HE RUNS INTO THE BOUNCER—JESUS

These scriptures refer to why the devil cannot come and request (using Adam's authority and permission) to sift God's kids anymore! Jesus is the Last Adam, and He took back the access once given to the devil by the first Adam.

Neither trials like the ones Job had to endure, nor the way Peter was sifted, are options on the table like they once were. Jesus slapped that system around and took back the reins. Today, the devil has access through the mind and by persuasion. To have access to tempt an individual, he needs their agreement and permission. Regarding Jesus' part, He labeled that door *Access Denied!*

Lucifer never had a tempter. He fell on his own doing—sin was found in him. As a result, he is not redeemable; no one tempted him, therefore, there was no one to rescue him or to punish him. He became "self-aware" and wanted worship, glory, and his egotistical ambitions. Adam and Eve had a tempter—Satan.

Jesus likewise, only in an entirely different field of significance, found *no intercessor for Him!* He had to discover His righteousness to sustain Him while tempted by the devil. Jesus realized Adam had failed, humankind had failed, and even Abraham wasn't going to make the cut, so God had no one to swear by—so He swore by Himself in a covenant. Dear reader, we should take a moment and thank God for His goodness!

Jesus was sustained by His righteousness; this overqualified Him to become the ultimate intercessor!

> *He saw that there was no man, and wondered that there was no intercessor; therefore His own arm brought salvation for Him; and His own righteousness, it sustained Him.*
>
> —Isaiah 59:16

Today, He sits at God's right hand, making intercession for us (*see* Romans 8:34). By making intercession for us, He intercepts the "accuser" of the brethren, who accuses the children of God day and night. God must have heard it when Adam gave his keys and access to the "accuser." It must have been wonderful when Jesus returned to heaven with the keys Adam gave up. Can you imagine Adam walking over and hugging Jesus for what He did?

Jesus' intercession is to stop the devil. Jesus is seated at the right hand of the Father as an eternal reminder that we are saved and we are in Him. This brings us to the point of intercession for the people of God. There is no ministry of intercession; however, the ability to intercede has been made available to all believers.

INTERCESSION IS A PRAYER THAT BRINGS REAL CHANGE

Prayer and intercession are powerful weapons, a higher form of intensity, in which believers throw the authority God gave them around in the spirit realm.

> *Likewise the Spirit also helps in our weaknesses. For we do not know what we should pray for as we ought, but the Spirit Himself makes intercession for us with groanings which cannot be uttered.*
>
> —Romans 8:26

Intercession doesn't take "No" for an answer. Intercession prayers—mixed with faith, Holy Spirit-led commands, and praying in the Spirit—say to the *mountain* or the *fight*, "No, you move!" Romans 8:26 says, "The Spirit Himself makes intercession for us with groanings which cannot be uttered." When going deep into prayer and intercession, there is a place in the Spirit where you can tap into that groaning. We can join in with Him and intercede through these Holy Spirit prayers for the Church. Sometimes, you will not know what you are praying for through intercession. You might be praying for someone on the other side of the world, and all you know is that you are joining with the Holy Spirit, praying in tongues, and agreeing with what He wants to accomplish. He needs you more than you realize. *Intercessory prayer is giving God a natural voice to speak with authority and declare His will through you.*

PRAY TO THE LORD OF THE HARVEST

One practical prayer of intercession is to pray to the Lord of the harvest, asking for laborers. God needs you to intercede on behalf of a dying world. Intercession is a *go-between* prayer. It makes tactical requests for those who need to hear the gospel, and you know you cannot be the one. Families are sometimes the hardest ones to reach because of familiarity. Praying to the Lord of the harvest to send laborers is a wonderful intercession, as it permits the Lord to act in a natural arena. When you pray and request or allow the Holy Spirit to pray through you with tongues and groanings, you are giving the Lord permission to have His will done on earth as it is in Heaven.

> *Therefore pray the Lord of the harvest to send out laborers into His harvest.*
>
> —Matthew 9:38

XERXES

Queen Esther's appeal to Xerxes was a form of intercession, but it was really Mordecai who was the intercessor. In a sense, Mordecai was the one who initiated Esther's action to save her nation. It was a form of sending laborers out into the fields, as Jesus said. Laborers go where you cannot. Mordecai knew what needed to be done, so he interceded by influencing a laborer—Esther.

> *So it was, when the king saw Queen Esther standing in the court, that she found favor in his sight, and the king held out to Esther the golden scepter that was in his hand. Then Esther went near and touched the top of the scepter.*
>
> —Esther 5:2

The background is important to realize the gravity of what Esther was risking. King Xerxes had a very unreliable personality. Gracious, kind, and given to sudden acts of rage and outbursts, he could become fiercely terrifying. This is commonly thought to be the same king personified in the movie *300* as the enormous god-king who fought with those three hundred Spartans, which history knows as the Battle of Thermopylae.

Three hundred Spartans held off an enormous Persian army by positioning themselves at the Hot Gates, a narrow passageway into their lands. (An interesting little-known historical possibility is that the Spartans were actually Jewish.)

Xerxes was notorious enough to make modern cinema because of his larger-than-life manic antics. An example of his behavior comes from history at a time when his enormous army was marching from Sardis to an area called Abydos. An important harbor of the day was located where he had built two bridges. Each bridge reached roughly 1,300 meters across. However, before Xerxes' army could utilize the bridges, a storm rose up and destroyed them both! History says Xerxes was enraged and had those responsible for building the bridges beheaded. A colorful addition to this story is that it's been said the furious king had fetters thrown into the strait and ordered for the sea to receive three hundred whiplashes! He also went as far as to have the sea branded with red-hot irons and commanded his soldiers to shout at that same water.

Esther was supposed to lay her life on the line with this same king. Her life was on the line with a madman who had breathtaking anger-management issues. However, it was her act of intercession that saved an entire nation.

4. GIVING THANKS

The Greek word used here is *eucharistia*. It conveys gratefulness and worship with gratitude to God. Gratefulness is when it's always on your lips to praise God!

> *Let the saints be joyful in glory; let them sing aloud on their beds.* [6] *Let the high praises of God be in their mouth, and a two-edged sword in their hand,* [7] *to execute vengeance on the nations, and punishments on the peoples;* [8] *to bind their kings with chains, and their nobles with fetters of iron;* [9] *to execute on them the written judgment—this honor have all His saints. Praise the LORD!*
>
> —Psalm 149:5-9

Praise is in the prayer spectrum and causes spiritual movement. Notice what happens here in Psalm 149. Singing praise leads to governmental authority! A conversation could be made that this is in reference to praise and the written Word of God. We know Scripture is referred to as the sword of the Spirit, and here we see the combination of those two leads to justice and governmental change. Praise mixed with the Word of God creates a space of authority, which is an honor for all His saints![1]

PUNISHING THE DARKNESS

This section on prayer, specifically the spiritual warfare prayers, is a selection of notes I have assembled. My family and I use these notes often when we pray together.

According to the Word of God, how a person prays can move mountains and break strongholds. I desire to equip you to thrive and win every battle the enemy throws your way.

Because of our covenant with God the Father through the blood of Jesus, we can use the Word of God combined with faith to face the devil head-on and win every time. One way we do so is to pray His Word. If you ever wonder what God's will is, pray His Word over any situation, and you will know what His will is concerning the matter.

For example, when facing any difficulty, pray out John 10:10, which says, "The thief does not come except to steal, and to kill, and to destroy. I have come that they may have life, and that they may have it more abundantly."

You could pray this way, "Lord, I know the difficulty I'm facing is not from You, for it is the enemy who comes to steal, kill, and destroy. I see in Your Word that You have come to give me life, and to give it more abundantly. In Jesus' name, I agree with Your Word for abundant life! By faith, I receive an abundance of life, and the God quality of life right now in the name of Jesus!"

When facing challenges in the world around you and the pressures of society, you can read this scripture and pray.

EFFECTIVE PRAYING

> *...The effective, fervent prayer of a righteous man avails much.*
>
> —James 5:16

The righteous should be armed with effective prayer. Effective means they know how to pray properly, but notice it says fervently. This word "fervently" means to *put forth power, to be at work, or to be self-operative.* When you know how to pray and exercise it fervently, you will accomplish much!

> *Who gave Himself for our sins, that He might deliver us from this present evil age, according to the will of our God and Father.*
>
> —Galatians 1:4

The following is a prayer to pray with this scripture:

> Lord, according to Galatians 1:4, I thank You that it is Your will that I will be delivered from this present evil age. So right now, I line up with Your will for my life and declare deliverance from every wicked thing in this present time. In Jesus' mighty name!

> *But the Lord is faithful, who shall establish you and guard you from the evil one.*
>
> —2 Thessalonians 3:3

I declare that the Lord is faithful, and He is establishing me right now and will guard me from the evil one!

Who shall separate us from the love of Christ? Shall tribulation, or distress, or persecution, or famine, or nakedness, or peril, or sword? [36] *As it is written: "For Your sake we are killed all day long; We are accounted as sheep for the slaughter."* [37] *Yet in all these things we are more than conquerors through Him who loved us.* [38] *For I am persuaded that neither death nor life, nor angels nor principalities nor powers, nor things present nor things to come,* [39] *nor height nor depth, nor any other created thing, shall be able to separate us from the love of God which is in Christ Jesus our Lord.*

—Romans 8:35-39

I thank You, Lord, that nothing can separate me from Your love! Today, in Jesus' name, I am more than a conqueror through You because You love me!

I can do all things through Christ who strengthens me.

—Philippians 4:13

I can do all things today through Christ who strengthens me. Today, I walk in Your ability, Lord.

The eternal God is your refuge, and underneath are the everlasting arms; He will thrust out the enemy from before you, and will say, "Destroy!"

—Deuteronomy 33:27

You, eternal God, are my refuge, and underneath me are Your everlasting arms. Today, I declare You are thrusting the enemy from before me, and I say the works of darkness will be destroyed in my life!

God is our refuge and strength, a very present help in trouble. [2] *Therefore we will not fear, even though the earth be removed, and though the mountains be carried into the midst of the sea;* [3] *though its waters roar and be troubled, though the mountains shake with its swelling. Selah.*

—Psalm 46:1-3

God, You are my refuge and strength, and You are very present in all that I face today. Therefore, I declare this day that I have no fear regardless of what may happen on earth. You are with me, and I trust in You.

The name of the LORD is a strong tower; the righteous run to it and are safe.

—Proverbs 18:10

I thank You, Lord, that Your name is a strong tower for me. I run to You in prayer and devotion right now, and I declare that I am safe.

And he said, "O man greatly beloved, fear not! Peace be to you; be strong, yes, be strong!" So when he spoke to me I was strengthened, and said, "Let my lord speak, for you have strengthened me."

—Daniel 10:19

Today, I declare I am greatly beloved and will not fear. I receive the peace You have given me. I declare in You I am strong; I receive Your strength. Speak to me today, Sir, for Your strength is upon me.

But those who wait on the LORD shall renew their strength; they shall mount up with wings like eagles, they shall run and not be weary, they shall walk and not faint.

—Isaiah 40:31

Right now I declare that because I wait on You, Sir, that my strength is renewed. I have vision and sight for my life and have Your supernatural energy to accomplish everything I need to do today.

Fear not, for I am with you; be not dismayed, for I am your God. I will strengthen you, yes, I will help you, I will uphold you with My righteous right hand.

—Isaiah 41:10

Because You are with me, I will not fear, nor will I be discouraged. In You, I receive strength. Thank You for helping and upholding me in Your righteous right hand.

The LORD is my rock and my fortress and my deliverer; my God, my strength, in whom I will trust; my shield and the horn of my salvation, my stronghold.

—Psalm 18:2

Lord, You are my rock and my fortress; You are my deliverer, my God, and my strength. Today, I put all my trust in You. You are my protection and the One who gives me authority. I am safe in Your protection.

The LORD is my light and my salvation; whom shall I fear? The LORD is the strength of my life; of whom shall I be afraid? [3] *… Though an army may encamp against me, my heart shall not fear; though war may rise against me, in this I will be confident.* [4] *One thing I have desired of the LORD, that will I seek: That I may dwell in the house of the LORD all the days of my life, to behold the beauty of the LORD, and to inquire in His temple.* [5] *For in the time of trouble He shall hide me in His pavilion; in the secret place of His tabernacle He shall hide me; He shall set me high upon a rock.*

—Psalm 27:1, 3-5

Lord, You are my light, which is my revelatory understanding. You are also my salvation from death, hell, and the grave. I fear nothing because You are with me. No matter what I face today, my heart will not fear because I know You are with me. I worship You, great God of heaven, for in the time of trouble You always hide me in Your safety.

Casting all your care upon Him, for He cares for you.

—1 Peter 5:7

Today, Lord, I cast all my cares—everything—upon You because I know You care for me and love me.

Let not your heart be troubled; you believe in God, believe also in Me.

—John 14:1

I take responsibility to not allow my heart to be troubled, for I believe in You, Sir, and in Jesus Christ my Lord.

And let the peace of God rule in your hearts, to which also you were called in one body; and be thankful.

—Colossians 3:15

Today, I give peace full rein in my heart, and I take my place in the body of Christ in Your service. Thank You, Jesus!

Peace I leave with you, My peace I give to you; not as the world gives do I give to you. Let not your heart be troubled, neither let it be afraid.

—John 14:27

Thank You, Jesus, that I have the peace You give living in me. I do not fear what the world fears, nor in the way they fear. I am not troubled nor afraid. In Jesus' name.

Be strong and of good courage, do not fear nor be afraid of them; for the LORD your God, He is the One who goes with you. He will not leave you nor forsake you.

—Deuteronomy 31:6

By faith, I declare I am strong and full of courage. I refuse to walk in fear or be afraid of any person. Thank You that You are my God! Thank You for going with me today and that You, Sir, will never leave me nor forsake me.

For God has not given us a spirit of fear, but of power and of love and of a sound mind.

—2 Timothy 1:7

I declare that I have no spirit of fear. Your power, love, and Your sound mind are working in me right now.

He who dwells in the secret place of the Most High shall abide under the shadow of the Almighty. [2] *I will say of the LORD, "He is my refuge and my fortress; my God, in Him I will trust."* [3] *Surely He shall deliver you from the snare of the fowler and from the perilous pestilence.* [4] *He shall cover you with His feathers, and under His wings you shall take refuge; His truth shall be your shield and buckler.* [5] *You shall not be afraid of the terror by night, nor of the arrow that flies by day,* [6] *nor of the pestilence that walks in darkness, nor of the destruction that lays waste at noonday.* [7] *A thousand may fall at your side, and ten thousand at your right hand; but it shall not come near you.* [8] *Only with your eyes shall you look, and see the reward of the wicked.* [9] *Because you have made the LORD, who is my refuge, even the Most High, your dwelling place,* [10] *no evil shall befall you, nor shall any plague come near your dwelling;* [11] *For He shall give His angels charge over you, to keep you in all your ways.* [12] *In their hands they shall bear you up, lest you dash your foot against a stone.* [13] *You shall tread upon the lion and the cobra, the young lion and the serpent you shall trample underfoot.* [14] *"Because he has set his love upon Me, therefore I will deliver him; I will set him on high, because he has known My name.* [15] *He shall call upon Me, and I will answer him; I will be with him in trouble; I will deliver him and honor him.* [16] *With long life I will satisfy him, and show him My salvation."*

—Psalm 91:1-16

For the following prayers, on the blanks fill in your name or the name of those you are praying for:

____________________ who dwells in the secret place of the Most High shall abide under the shadow of the Almighty. [2] ____________________ will say of the LORD, "He is my refuge and my fortress; my God, in Him ____________________ will trust." [3] Surely He shall deliver ____________________ from the snare of the fowler and from the perilous pestilence. [4]

He shall cover ____________________ with His feathers, and
under His wings ________________________ shall take refuge;
His truth shall be ____________________ shield and buckler. [5]
____________________ shall not be afraid of the terror by night,
nor of the arrow that flies by day, [6] nor of the pestilence that walks in
darkness, nor of the destruction that lays waste at noonday. [7] A thousand may fall at ____________________ side, and ten thousand
at ____________________ right hand; but it shall not come
near ____________________. [8] Only with ________________
eyes shall ________________ look, and see the reward
of the wicked. [9] Because ____________________
have made the LORD, who is ______________ refuge,
even the Most High, ____________________ dwelling place, [10] no evil shall befall ____________________,
nor shall any plague come near ________________
dwelling; [11] For He shall give His angels charge over
____________________, to keep ________________
in all ________________ ways. [12] In their hands they shall
bear________________ up, lest ________________
dash your foot against a stone. [13] ________________
shall tread upon the lion and the cobra, the young lion and the
serpent you shall trample underfoot. [14] "Because he has set his
love upon ____________________, therefore I will deliver
____________________; I will set ____________________
on high, because ____________________ has known
My name. [15] ________________________ shall call
upon Me, and I will answer ____________________;
I will be with ________________ in trouble; I will deliver
________________ and honor ________________. [16]
With long life I will satisfy ____________________, and show
____________________ My salvation."

Do not be afraid of sudden terror, nor of trouble from the wicked when it comes; [26] For the LORD will be your confidence, and will keep your foot from being caught.

—Proverbs 3:25-26

In Jesus' name, I am not afraid, not of sudden terror or of any form of trouble from any form of wickedness. You, Sir, are my confidence, and I thank You for keeping my foot from being caught in any way.

Thus says the LORD to His anointed, to Cyrus, whose right hand I have held—to subdue nations before him and loose the armor of kings, to open before him the double doors, so that the gates will not be shut: [2] *"I will go before you and make the crooked places straight; I will break in pieces the gates of bronze and cut the bars of iron.* [3] *I will give you the treasures of darkness and hidden riches of secret places, that you may know that I, the LORD, who call you by your name, Am the God of Israel."*

—Isaiah 45:1-3

Thus says the LORD to ____________, to ____________, whose right hand I have held—to subdue nations before ________ and loose the armor of kings, to open before him the double doors, so that the gates will not be shut: [2] "I will go before ____________ and make the crooked places straight; I will break in pieces the gates of bronze and cut the bars of iron. [3] I will give ____________ the treasures of darkness and hidden riches of secret places, that ____________ may know that I, the LORD, who call ____________ by your name, Am the God of Israel."

Yea, though I walk through the valley of the shadow of death, I will fear no evil; for You are with me; Your rod and Your staff, they comfort me. [5] *You prepare a table before me in the presence of my enemies; You anoint my head with oil; my cup runs over.* [6] *Surely goodness and mercy shall follow me all the days of my life; and I will dwell in the house of the LORD forever.*

—Psalm 23:4-6

Yea, though ________________ walk through the valley of the shadow of death, ________________ will fear no evil; for You are with ____________; Your rod and Your staff, they comfort ____________. [5] You prepare a table before ____________ in the presence of ____________ enemies; You anoint

____________ head with oil; ________________ cup runs over. [6] Surely goodness and mercy shall follow _____________ all the days of ______________ life; and _______________ will dwell in the house of the LORD forever.

Cast your burden on the LORD, and He shall sustain you; He shall never permit the righteous to be moved.

—Psalm 55:22

I cast all my burdens and troubles onto You right now, Lord. Thank You that You sustain me! I declare that because I am in You I shall never be moved.

Be anxious for nothing, but in everything by prayer and supplication, with thanksgiving, let your requests be made known to God; [7] and the peace of God, which surpasses all understanding, will guard your hearts and minds through Christ Jesus.

—Philippians 4:6-7

In Jesus' name, today, I will be anxious for nothing at all! I lean into prayer with You, Lord, letting You know exactly what I need. I now receive Your peace which goes beyond my understanding and declare that peace is guarding my heart and mind through Christ Jesus, my Lord.

But now, thus says the LORD, who created you, O Jacob, and He who formed you, O Israel: "Fear not, for I have redeemed you; I have called you by your name; you are Mine. [2] When you pass through the waters, I will be with you; and through the rivers, they shall not overflow you. When you walk through the fire, you shall not be burned, nor shall the flame scorch you.

—Isaiah 43:1-2

But now, thus says the LORD, who created, __________ O _________, and He who formed you, ___________: "Fear not, for I have redeemed __________; I have called

_______________ by your name; _______________ is Mine. [2] When _______________ pass through the waters, I will be with _______________; and through the rivers, they shall not overflow _______________. When _______________ walk through the fire, _______________ shall not be burned, nor shall the flame scorch _______________.

Blessed be the God and Father of our Lord Jesus Christ, the Father of mercies and God of all comfort, [4] who comforts us in all our tribulation, that we may be able to comfort those who are in any trouble, with the comfort with which we ourselves are comforted by God.

—2 Corinthians 1:3-4

Blessed be the God and Father of our Lord Jesus Christ, the Father of mercies and God of all comfort, [4] who comforts _______________ in all _______________ tribulation, that _______________ may be able to comfort those who are in any trouble, with the comfort with which _______________ is comforted by God.

Though I walk in the midst of trouble, You will revive me; You will stretch out Your hand against the wrath of my enemies, and Your right hand will save me.

—Psalm 138:7

Though _______________ walk in the midst of trouble, You will revive _______________; You will stretch out Your hand against the wrath of _______________ enemies, and Your right hand will save _______________.

Many are the afflictions of the righteous, but the LORD delivers him out of them all.

—Psalm 34:19

Many are the afflictions of the righteous, but the LORD delivers _______________ out of them all.

For assuredly, I say to you, whoever says to this mountain, "Be removed and be cast into the sea," and does not doubt in his heart, but believes that those things he says will be done, he will have whatever he says. [24] *Therefore I say to you, whatever things you ask when you pray, believe that you receive them, and you will have them.*

—Mark 11:23-24

For assuredly, I say to, ____________________ who says to this mountain, "Be removed and be cast into the sea," and (because) ____________________ does not doubt in ______________ heart, but believes that those things ______________ says will be done, ________________ will have whatever ____________________ says. Therefore I say to you, whatever things ________________ ask when ______________ prays, believe that ____________________ receives them, and____________________ will have them.

So the Lord said, "If you have faith as a mustard seed, you can say to this mulberry tree, 'Be pulled up by the roots and be planted in the sea,' and it would obey you."

—Luke 17:6

So the Lord said, "If __________________________ have faith as a mustard seed, __________________________ can say to this mulberry tree, 'Be pulled up by the roots and be planted in the sea,' and it would obey ____________________."

SERVANTS OF FIRE SCRIPTURAL DECLARATIONS

This section is from my book, *Servants of Fire*. Releasing angels by the Word of God is a potent force when executing spiritual warfare.

And of the angels He says: "Who makes His angels spirits and His ministers a flame of fire."

—Hebrews 1:7

Are they not all ministering spirits sent forth to minister for those who will inherit salvation?

—Hebrews 1:14

Lord, I thank You that You make Your angels spirits and ministering flames of fire for my sake and the sake of my loved ones.

The voice of the LORD divides the flames of fire.

—Psalm 29:7

I thank You, Lord, that when I speak any promise from Your Word (out loud), Your flames of fire are divided into ranks for assignment.

Bless the LORD, you His angels, who excel in strength, who do His word, heeding the voice of His word. [21] *Bless the LORD, all you His hosts, you ministers of His, who do His pleasure.* [22] *Bless the LORD, all His works, in all places of His dominion. Bless the LORD, O my soul!*

—Psalm 103:20-22

Lord, I thank You that Your Word is alive and active in me, that I can speak Your Word, and that the angels will heed Your Word and respond.

Thank You that Your angels do Your pleasure for my sake and my family, and that it pleases You when we speak the Word to activate angels. Right now, in Jesus' name, I declare (insert your prayer) that Your servants of fire heed it and do Your pleasure over my life!

Let them shout for joy and be glad, who favor my righteous cause; and let them say continually, "Let the LORD be magnified, who has pleasure in the prosperity of His servant."

—Psalm 35:27

Thank You, Lord, that according to Psalm 103:21, angels do Your pleasure. Psalm 35:27 says You have pleasure in my prosperity. So right now, in Jesus' name, I agree with God's prosperity over my life and that angels are being sent out to fulfill Your pleasure over me.

Behold, I send an Angel before you to keep you in the way and to bring you into the place which I have prepared.

—Exodus 23:20

Behold, I send an Angel before you to keep and guard you on the way and to bring you to the place I have prepared.

—Exodus 23:20 AMPC

This scripture is the release of angelic preparation for where you are currently and where you are headed. Use it when praying over your life and future plans, as well as in prayers about relocating to new locations, taking trips, or embarking on new ventures.

Thank You, Lord, that You have placed an angel before me to keep and guard me on my way to the place that You have prepared for me.

Then the LORD sent an angel who cut down every mighty man of valor, leader, and captain in the camp of the king of Assyria. So he returned shamefaced to his own land. And when he had gone into the temple of his god, some of his own offspring struck him down with the sword there.

—2 Chronicles 32:21

This powerful prayer scripture is to stop the enemy's attacks on any particular situation.

Lord, I call forth Your angels to cut down every assignment, influence, or evil persuasion against You that is attacking my life. That evil plans would be cut down, the plans of darkness would fail, and the thing fighting against me would be turned away shamefaced and sent back to where it came from.

The angel of the LORD encamps all around those who fear Him, and delivers them.

—Psalm 34:7

This prayer is for the divine angelic protection of those who fear the Lord.

> Lord, I thank You that the angel of the Lord is encamping around me and my family and that they deliver us from all our adversaries.

For He shall give His angels charge over you, to keep you in all your ways.
12 *In their hands they shall bear you up, lest you dash your foot against a stone.*

—Psalm 91:11-12

This scripture has three points of angelic help attached to it.

1. *Angels taking charge of you* means they have permission and the responsibility to intervene in circumstances, like a person reaching over and grabbing a steering wheel to correct a car.
2. *Keep you*—this means they are always present and continue watching over you to ensure nothing goes wrong with you.
3. They have permission to *reach out with their hands*—a reference to physically altering a circumstance to rescue or alter something for your benefit. Similar to when Peter had shackles removed from his hands and feet, or the gates to the prison opened by themselves, and Peter walked out. This was the doing of angelic hands.

> Thank You, Lord, for charging Your angels over me and my family, and that they keep us in all our ways, that Your angels will bear us up, and thank You that we won't get hurt in the process.

Nebuchadnezzar spoke, saying, "Blessed be the God of Shadrach, Meshach, and Abed-Nego, who sent His Angel and delivered His servants who trusted in Him, and they have frustrated the king's word, and yielded their bodies, that they should not serve nor worship any god except their own God!"

—Daniel 3:28

A promise is found here to foil the plans of bad leadership or institutions that set out to do you harm. Angels can frustrate the wrong laws or evil commands for your protection.

Lord, I call forth Your angels to come and deliver me from every evil situation. I pray that they would frustrate the words of the enemy against me.

And He was there in the wilderness forty days, tempted by Satan, and was with the wild beasts; and the angels ministered to Him.

—Mark 1:13

This scripture carries the idea that angels can refresh you.

Lord, I call forth Your ministering angels to minister to me, my family, and my loved ones.

Or do you think that I cannot now pray to My Father, and He will provide Me with more than twelve legions of angels?

—Matthew 26:53

This powerful scripture holds an understanding of a high-level intervention. You can pray for high-level angelic assistance! As He is, so are we in this world. If Jesus could pray it, so can we.

Thank You, Lord, that just like Jesus knew He could pray and ask You to provide Him with many angels, we have that same ability, through Jesus and Your Word, to call forth the assistance of Your angels. In Jesus' name, I call forth Your heavenly legions to assist me in every circumstance!

But at night an angel of the Lord opened the prison doors and brought them out, and said, [20] "Go, stand in the temple and speak to the people all the words of this life."

—Acts 5:19-20

Now behold, an angel of the Lord stood by him, and a light shone in the prison; and he struck Peter on the side and raised him up, saying, "Arise quickly!" And his chains fell off his hands.

—Acts 12:7

Suddenly there was a great earthquake, so that the foundations of the prison were shaken; and immediately all the doors were opened and everyone's chains were loosed.

—Acts 16:26

Thank You, Lord, that in moments of desperation, trials, and hardships, You send Your angels to help me in many ways to get out of every situation that is not of You.

I call forth Your angels to go to the aid of (person's name) and help them in whatever way the angels can, so that (name) can get freedom from their situation.

For there stood by me this night an angel of the God to whom I belong and whom I serve.

—Acts 27:23

Thank You, Lord, that You have sent Your angel to stand by my side through every difficulty.[2]

COMBATING SPIRITUAL FORCES

Assuredly, I say to you, whatever you bind on earth will be bound in heaven, and whatever you loose on earth will be loosed in heaven. [19] *Again I say to you that if two of you agree on earth concerning anything that they ask, it will be done for them by My Father in heaven.*

—Matthew 18:18–19

In Jesus' name, I bind all forms of evil and demonic power in my life and the lives of my loved ones. I agree with Your Word, Lord, that because I bind these things, they are bound in heaven and on earth. In Jesus' name, I loose the blessing and Your will over my life and my loved ones. Every demonic force is rendered powerless now in Jesus' name!

For the weapons of our warfare are not carnal but mighty in God for pulling down strongholds, [5] *casting down arguments and every high thing that exalts itself against the knowledge of God, bringing every thought into captivity to the obedience of Christ.*

—2 Corinthians 10:4-5

Right now, in Jesus' name, I activate Your spiritual weapons over my life to pull down strongholds. Strongholds come down in Jesus' name! By casting aside every argument and thought that exalts itself against the knowledge of God, I take the authority You have given me, Jesus, and release the will of God in my life right now.

Behold, I give you the authority to trample on serpents and scorpions, and over all the power of the enemy, and nothing shall by any means hurt you.

—Luke 10:19

I exercise the authority You have given me, Jesus, right now, to trample on snakes and scorpions, or any demonic force in my sphere. I take authority right now over all the power of the enemy in Jesus' name and declare that the will of God is happening in my life now.

He has delivered us from the power of darkness and conveyed us into the kingdom of the Son of His love.

—Colossians 1:13

I thank You, God, that You have delivered me by the power of Jesus' blood! Every power of darkness cannot hold or fight against me today in Jesus' name, for I am in the kingdom of Your Son Jesus Christ!

REFLECT, REPENT, AND BE SAVED

Now may be a good time to reflect on your relationship with the living God. If you have not made Jesus the Lord and Savior of your life, please consider doing that now.

"...the word is near you, in your mouth and in your heart" (that is, the word of faith which we preach): [9] *that if you confess with your mouth the Lord Jesus and believe in your heart that God has raised Him from the dead, you will be saved.* [10] *For with the heart one believes unto righteousness, and with the mouth confession is made unto salvation.* [11] *For the Scripture says, "Whoever believes on Him will not be put to shame."* ... [13] *For "whoever calls on the name of the Lord shall be saved."*

—Romans 10:8-11, 13

God has done everything by His grace and mercy to provide for your salvation. Accepting Jesus as your Lord and Savior is as simple as believing in your heart (being fully persuaded) that He died for you, rose from the dead, and is now seated at the right hand of God. If you believe, then confess this aloud:

Lord, I confess that I have sinned and need a Savior. I believe in my heart, and do not doubt, that You, Jesus, died for me to forgive me of all of my sins—past, present, and future. I believe God raised You from the dead, and You are seated at His right hand. I call on the name of the Lord. I am saved!

Welcome to the family of God!

SECTION 5

MECHANISMS OF AN ANTICHRIST AGENDA

CHAPTER FOURTEEN

WEAPONS OF MASS DECEPTION: UFOS, AI, THE SINGULARITY, PROJECT BLUE BEAM, AND THE CLIMATE RELIGION

And there will be great earthquakes in various places, and famines and pestilences; and there will be fearful sights and great signs from heaven.

—Luke 21:11

And there will be signs in the sun, in the moon, and in the stars; and on the earth distress of nations, with perplexity, the sea and the waves roaring;
26 *men's hearts failing them from fear and the expectation of those things which are coming on the earth, for the powers of the heavens will be shaken.*

—Luke 21:25-26

In this chapter, I outline a few current issues in the culture that, in the eyes of many, appear to carry a nefarious agenda. These are listed and defined to bring an awareness for you, dear reader, to discern and pray about. Although there are many additional issues we face as a society, it is the Church's responsibility to walk informed and with the Holy Spirit's power toward rising issues and entities of wickedness. Prayerfully consider what is listed in this chapter as a reference and a point of prayer.

Jesus' comments on the end of the age are startling. His statements in Luke 21:11 say, "...and there will be fearful sights and great signs from heaven...."

MONSTERS?

My friend, who is known for his work in the Greek, Rick Renner, observes in his masterpiece, *Fallen Angels, Giants, Monsters & The World Before the Flood,* that the original Greek word *phobētron,* which is translated as "fearful sights," is the word Jesus used in Luke 21:11; it is a word that was used by ancient Greeks to describe *monsters*.[1] Therefore, we must ask: What would have been considered a "monster" at the time Jesus used this word and prophesied that "fearful sights" (monsters) would appear at the end of this age?

Venturing into the realm of conjecture is the only way to imagine what Jesus was specifically referring to. We can examine the current state of the world along with its technologies and advancements, which may have serious spiritual implications. In light of what Jesus said in Luke 21, regarding fearful sights, and His statement in verse 26 that men's hearts would fail them from fear and the expectation of those things which are coming on the earth, it is worthwhile to consider several issues we are facing as a culture.

Much of what we will examine are aspects that most people wouldn't associate with spiritual warfare issues; however, they truly are. We must be aware of them and determine our course of action. Most importantly, we must understand that our response as the *Ekklesia* is crucial to the survival of the culture as we know it.

Remember, as believers in the One True Living God, what we can accomplish is monumental when we understand who we are and what we can restrain or alter as God's holy people. The world will one day embrace the issues we are about to explore, in part or the whole. When the Antichrist comes into world power, rogue technologies, deception in the heavens, and the various controversial challenges we face today will all be mechanized to fit the narrative of the Antichrist. Today, it is encouraging to know that, according to Paul the apostle, a restraining force holds the full manifestation of evil at bay; as such, we can say to these evil things, "Not here, not now, and not on our watch!" I believe that the Church is the restraining force on earth.

> *And now you know what is restraining, that he may be revealed in his own time.*
>
> —2 Thessalonians 2:6

ARTIFICIAL INTELLIGENCE AND THE SINGULARITY

> *And he deceives those who dwell on the earth by those signs which he was granted to do in the sight of the beast, telling those who dwell on the earth to make an image to the beast who was wounded by the sword and lived.*
> 15 *He was granted power to give breath to the image of the beast, that the image of the beast should both speak and cause as many as would not worship the image of the beast to be killed.*
>
> —Revelation 13:14-15

AI is well on its way to becoming a false religion that could eventually lead to what is known as the singularity. It is not far-fetched to consider that AI might be the mechanism by which breath and animation are given to the image of the beast in Revelation 13:15. Among the many concerns about AI is the event many believe is imminent, if not already underway—the singularity.

THE SINGULARITY

> *But you, Daniel, shut up the words, and seal the book until the time of the end; many shall run to and fro, and knowledge shall increase.*
>
> —Daniel 12:4

The singularity, defined in the context of artificial intelligence (AI), refers to a hypothetical future point where AI surpasses human intelligence and begins a cycle of self-improvement that humans cannot predict or control, leading to profound and unpredictable changes in human civilization. This concept was popularized by American science fiction author[2] and computer scientist Vernor Vinge,[3] who described it as an event where the machines grow so advanced that humans are forced into a societal and existential crisis.

MERGING OF MAN AND MACHINE

Ray Kurzweil, a renowned inventor and futurist, predicts the singularity, a phase in which technology changes so rapidly that it's impossible to predict what will happen next. Yet Kurzweil predicts the singularity will occur in the next 20 years. He envisions a future where human and machine intelligence merge, leading to profound changes in society, the economy, and human life itself. Kurzweil's predictions are based on the exponential growth of technology, particularly in computing power, biotechnology, nanotechnology, and artificial intelligence.

He believes that in the very near future, artificial intelligence will reach human-level intelligence. Within 20 years, human intelligence will be expanded a millionfold through nanobots and other technologies, enhancing our cognitive abilities and potentially leading to radical life extension and the reversal of aging. Further, Kurzweil believes topics such as rebuilding the world atom by atom with nanobots, reinventing intelligence by connecting our brains to the cloud, and the potential perils and benefits of biotechnology and nanotechnology will all be interconnected as parallels of the singularity and artificial intelligence.

Despite the optimism, Kurzweil acknowledges the potential risks of these advancements and emphasizes the need for ongoing dialogue to address the challenges and concerns arising from these accelerating possibilities.[4]

A BRAVE NEW WORLD

Aldous Huxley's *Brave New World,* published in 1932, is a dystopian novel set in 2540 BC. The "Word State" is a technology-advanced society that values efficiency, stability, and happiness above all else. In this society, individuals are genetically engineered and conditioned from birth to fit into one of five castes: Alphas, Betas, Gammas, Deltas, and Epsilons, with each caste having specific roles and characteristics.[5]

Some believe Huxley's work is not simply a story but a manual for the wicked elite's plan for the future of civilization. Artificial Intelligence and the potential of the singularity would make all the potential of what Huxley wrote a much greater possibility.

THE GREAT ALIEN DECEPTION

> *And I saw three unclean spirits like frogs coming out of the mouth of the dragon, out of the mouth of the beast, and out of the mouth of the false prophet. 14 For they are spirits of demons, performing signs, which go out to the kings of the earth and of the whole world, to gather them to the battle of that great day of God Almighty.*
>
> —Revelation 16:13-14

In the last days, supernatural and paranormal events will become increasingly prevalent, culminating in a final deception. The UFO alien phenomena will be a major player in that. Revelation 16:13-14 may be speaking of alien-type creatures that will come upon the earth to deceive.

> *And there will be signs in the sun, in the moon, and in the stars; and on the earth distress of nations, with perplexity, the sea and the waves roaring; 26 men's hearts failing them from fear and the expectation of those things which are coming on the earth, for the powers of the heavens will be shaken.*
>
> —Luke 21:25-26

Looking at Luke 21 again, notice Jesus' words: "Men's hearts will fail them from fear and expectation of things which are coming on the earth." Then it reads, "The powers of the heavens will be shaken." The Bible doesn't specify what is coming upon the earth, but whatever it is will be observable and expected. Fear, to the point of a heart attack, will result from such events.

FALSIFIED ALIEN INVASION

One issue that we can consider is a falsified alien invasion or visitation. Paranormal encounters, hysteria around UFOs, and our growing culture of disclosure would undoubtedly point to this possibility. This does not mean that what is coming will not be real; it simply means we must deal with it according to Isaiah 8:12, which says, "...nor be afraid of their threats, nor be troubled."[6]

UFOs and the fascination with alien beings have reached a point where they have become a normalcy bias for most people. Not understanding what they are or what is happening regarding them presents a challenge for the average person and the highly educated. Once you grasp the greater force at work behind these controversial issues, the reaction becomes clear, and the answer remains the same: Jesus is Lord, and we are here to enforce His will and kingdom.

But what are UFOs?

UFOS ARE THREE THINGS

1. Whether governments or companies are involved in manufacturing it, it is a powerful technology that surpasses our understanding. Some have cited issues as far back as Nazi experimentation as the origins for next-generation tech many have seen in the sky.
2. Many consider deceptive technology combined with psychological operations, such as the famous "Project Blue Beam," a mechanism of control using UFOs, a Messianic visitation, or something else.
3. Real demonic or fallen angel activity manifesting in our skies due to permission by the tampering of wicked science through places like CERN and the Tower of Babel before it.

PROJECT BLUE BEAM

For false christs and false prophets will rise and show great signs and wonders to deceive, if possible, even the elect.

—Matthew 24:24

Let's address one of the issues that could be part of the greatest deception the world will face in the last days. "Project Blue Beam" may bring about this ultimate deception, which could involve, as Jesus warned, the potential to deceive even the elect.

A summary of Project Blue Beam by Canadian journalist and whistleblower Serge Monast: in short, Project Blue Beam is an alleged conspiracy theory that claims agencies, mainly NASA, are attempting to implement a New Age religion with the Antichrist at its head and start a New World Order via a technologically simulated Messianic Second Coming.

Monast's allegations were presented in 1994 and later published in his book *Project Blue Beam (NASA)*. Proponents of the theory allege that Monast and another unnamed journalist, who both died of heart attacks in 1996, were assassinated, and that the Canadian government kidnapped Monast's daughter to dissuade him from investigating Project Blue Beam.[7]

Monast states that the infamous NASA [National Aeronautics and Space Administration] Blue Beam Project has four different steps to implement the new age religion with the Antichrist at its head. We must remember that the new age religion is the foundation for the new world government, without which religion, the dictatorship of the new world order is completely impossible. Without a universal belief in the new age religion, the success of the new world order will be impossible! That is why some believe the Blue Beam Project is so important to them, but it has been so well hidden until now.[8]

MONAST'S WORK LISTS FOUR STAGES OF PROJECT BLUE BEAM

The following are the four purported stages, summarized from available sources:

1. Breakdown of Archaeological Knowledge: Engineered earthquakes would unearth fake artifacts to discredit major religions, particularly Christianity and Islam, by "proving" their doctrines false, weakening faith in traditional beliefs.[9]
2. Massive Sky Projections: Advanced holographic technology would project images of religious figures or extraterrestrial invasions tailored to cultural beliefs, creating a global spectacle to deceive populations and promote a new universal religion.[10]
3. Telepathic Communication and Mind Control: Using technology like radio wavelengths and possibly HAARP, elites would simulate divine or supernatural communication, manipulating thoughts to foster acceptance of the new world order.[11]

4. Staged Supernatural Events and Crises: Simulated miracles, alien invasions, or other crises would be orchestrated to instill fear, dismantle national identities and family structures, and solidify allegiance to a global authority.[12]

Critics of Monast argue that his claims lack credible evidence and are largely dismissed as speculative. The theory, derived from Monast's writings, has been linked to events such as an increase in drone sightings, but it remains unverified.

What is incredibly concerning is that a mass deception event, such as the possibility of a "Project Blue Beam," could indeed lead to a worldwide occurrence, placing control of the population in the hands of those orchestrating such a scenario.

GENDER CONFUSION

> *A woman shall not wear anything that pertains to a man, nor shall a man put on a woman's garment, for all who do so are an abomination to the LORD your God.*
>
> —Deuteronomy 22:5

What is it that causes people to have an identity crisis involving their very biology? Where does this confusion come from? To answer, we must realize there is nothing new under the sun. The notion of gender dysphoria and the religion of transgenderism has ties back to ancient times.

THE CULT OF CYBELE

During the early Church, a widespread movement was known as the Cybele cult, which included *men known as Galli who dressed as women.* These Galli were eunuch priests who castrated themselves as part of their initiation into the cult, and they were known for their effeminate dress and demeanor. They wore women's clothing and accessories, and some modern scholars interpret them as transgender.[13]

Although the Cult of Cybele is not directly mentioned by name in the Bible, her cult is referenced indirectly in some passages. For instance, in 1 Timothy 2, Paul's prohibition on a woman teaching or assuming authority over a man might be influenced by the radical ascetic practices associated with the Cybele cult, which included ritual castration.[14]

ELEUSIAN MYSTERY CULT

Along with the "mysteries of Cybele" (a name for the secret rites of the Cybele cult) are additional shared religious beliefs and practices, such as the "Eleusian mysteries" in Greece. In the Eleusian mysteries, men chemically castrated themselves by taking hemlock, a poisonous flowering plant.[15] Like physical castration, this practice also risked killing the man. It also cut a man off from having future offspring. This use of hemlock was so dangerous that it became expressly prohibited by Cornelius Sulla, a Roman general and statesman of the late Roman Republic.[16]

HISTORICAL REFERENCES TO THE CULT OF CYBELE

An ox-eating lion came to the cave-mouth; with the flat of his hand he struck the great timbrel he was carrying, and the whole cave rang with the din: the forest beast could not abide the holy booming of Kybele and raced quickly up the forested mountain, afraid of the goddess' half-woman servant [i.e., a eunuch priest]--who hung up [as a dedication] for Rheia these garments and yellow locks.

—Stesichorus, Fragment 59 (trans. Campbell, Vol. Greek Lyric III) (C7th to 6th B.C.)

Tossing my hair to honour Kybele to the sound of the Phrygian flute or in trailing robe, alas! To mourn Adonis [i.e. Attis], the slave of the goddess.

—Callimachus, Iambi Fragment 193 (trans. Trypanis) (Greek poet C3rd B.C.)

'But why do we call the self-castrated Galli, when the Gallic land is far from Phrygia?' 'Between,' she says, 'green Cybele and high Celaenae [in Phrygia] runs a stream of bad water named Gallus. Its taste causes madness. Keep away, if you want a healthy mind. Its

taste causes madness.' 'Aren't they ashamed,' I said, 'to place a herb salad before the Mistress? Or is there some cause?'

—Ovid, Fasti 4. 181 ff (trans. Boyle) (Roman poetry C1st B.C. to C1st A.D.) [The festival of the Meter Theon in Rome :] April 4 Megalensia Ludi Comitailis.

Our modern world has seen a shocking spike in transgenderism. It is highly preached in the world that the way people are born doesn't mean that's who they are supposed to be. So if a little boy wants to be a girl, the world says, "Get him on hormone blockers, put him in a dress, and change his name to a girl's name."

States are taking parental rights away, especially when it comes to their child's gender. If a child wants to be the opposite sex and they want to change their name or sex, some states are punishing parents if they refuse to consent to these changes. Sadly, this topic is so prevalent in schools, on television, and the government that it's becoming normalized.

The Antichrist spirit wants to continue the nefarious activity like the fallen angels did in Genesis 6, by perverting what God created. Could it be that these vile creatures, fallen angels and demons, are still so jealous of man that they want to destroy every process of God's natural plan for humanity? The answer is yes.

TRANSGENDERISM LEADS TO TRANSHUMANISM, ALL ROOTED IN TRANSGRESSION

Transhumanism, by definition, is the philosophical and scientific movement that advocates using current and emerging technologies, such as genetic engineering, cryonics, artificial intelligence (AI), and nanotechnology, to augment human capabilities and improve the human condition.[17] While transhumanism boasts the belief or theory that the human race can evolve beyond its current physical and mental limitations, especially using science and technology, all sounds noble. Yet, the purpose driving this is Luciferian in origin.

An example of transhumanism today would be these scientific practices of stem cell therapies, in vitro fertilization, brain chips, animal cloning, exoskeletons (e.g., robotic arms), artificial intelligence, and genomics or human genome editing.[18]

We are told of the tremendous benefits of transhumanism, such as brain chips inserted in the human brain to create a brain-computer interface (BCI). They record and transmit neural activity wirelessly, allowing users to control external devices like computers or smartphones through their thoughts. The chip aims to help individuals with paralysis or other neurological conditions regain control over their lives.

REACHING IMMORTALITY WITHOUT GOD

Why transhumanism? Scientists are on the search for immortality. Transhumanists have the term "Human Enhancement" or HE, and embrace the so-called three pillars of transhumanism:

1. *A superintelligent intellect* can radically outperform the best human brains in practically every field, including scientific creativity, general wisdom, and social skills.
2. *Super-longevity* means *extending human life.* The scientific goal is to achieve healthier, happier, and more productive years. The idea is that everybody should have the right to choose when and how to die—or not to die.
3. *Super-wellbeing* is based on the principles of bodily autonomy and procreative liberty. Using genetic medicine or embryonic screening to increase the probability of a healthy, happy, and what is called a "multiply talented child" is used as a justifiable application of parental reproductive freedom.[19]

Transhumanists are on a Luciferian path, purposefully or inadvertently attempting to become God and achieve immortality. Luciferian, as this was Satan's desire before he fell and after—to be like God.

> *For you [speaking of Satan] have said in your heart: "I will ascend into heaven, I will exalt my throne above the stars of God; I will also sit on the mount of the congregation on the farthest sides of the north; [14] I will ascend above the heights of the clouds,* ***I will be like the Most High.*** *"*
>
> —Isaiah 14:13-14

Satan has desired to be like God since the very beginning. He knows he will never be like God, but he will do his best to destroy what God has created. When there is a willing vessel ready to be used by him, he will make every effort to destroy the works of the Lord through corruption, lies, and perversion of God's purpose for humankind.

THE CLIMATE CHANGE RELIGION

For nation will rise against nation, and kingdom against kingdom. And there will be famines, pestilences, and earthquakes in various places.

—Matthew 24:7

The United Nations defines climate change as follows: Climate change refers to long-term shifts in temperatures and weather patterns.[20] However, when looking into the climate change narrative (once referred to as global warming), alarming facts and issues that counter the mainstream narrative arise. Climate change has been treated like a religion regarding the blind acceptance of it and the fierce defense of it.

COFOUNDER OF THE WEATHER CHANNEL

In a 2014 interview on CNN, John Coleman, cofounder of The Weather Channel, stated, "Climate change is not happening. There is no significant man-made global warming now, there hasn't been any in the past, and there is no reason to expect any in the future."[21]

When the host responded that there was a scientific consensus that global warming was real, Coleman responded that there is "no consensus in science that humans are causing climate change." He went on to call the notion of Climate Change "baloney." Of course, media outlets promptly condemned him for his comments.

POINTS TO CONSIDER ABOUT CLIMATE CHANGE

The notion that climate change is a hoax begins with the observation that Earth's climate has always been in flux, long before human activity could be blamed. Geological records indicate that warming and cooling cycles have spanned millions of years, driven by natural factors such as solar radiation, volcanic activity, and ocean currents. For instance, the Medieval Warm Period (roughly AD 950–1250) experienced temperatures comparable to or higher than those of today, followed by the Little Ice Age, all before the onset of industrial emissions.

The current warming trend, often attributed to human CO2 output, could be part of these natural cycles. Moreover, the emphasis on CO2 as a primary driver overlooks other potent forces, such as methane from natural sources or cosmic rays influencing cloud formation, which some scientists argue have a greater impact. The selective focus on anthropogenic causes feels like a narrative crafted to fit a preconceived agenda rather than a dispassionate analysis of all variables.

Next, the reliability of climate science itself comes under scrutiny when the data and models are examined. Temperature records are often adjusted—older readings are lowered, while modern ones are raised—creating an exaggerated warming trend.

THE CLIMATEGATE EMAILS

The infamous "Climategate" emails from 2009 revealed the unauthorized release of more than 1,000 emails and 3,000 documents from the University of East Anglia's Climatic Research Unit (CRU). These were hacked from a server in November 2009, just before the Copenhagen Climate Summit, and were used by climate change skeptics to allege scientific misconduct, data manipulation, and suppression of dissenting views by prominent climate scientists discussing ways to "hide the decline" in temperature data that didn't fit their models.

Climate models, meanwhile, are shown to consistently overpredict warming compared to observed temperatures, with many failing to account for natural variability or feedback mechanisms like cloud cover. These models are then used to justify apocalyptic predictions, despite their track record of inaccuracy. This and much more was uncovered in those 2009 emails. Columnist James Delingpole then popularized "Climategate" to frame the issue as a scandal.[22]

FUNDING AND POLITICAL MOTIVATION MUDDY THE WATERS REGARDING CLIMATE CHANGE

Funding and political pressures further complicate the situation: grants and careers depend on reinforcing the narrative of the climate crisis, while dissenting voices are marginalized or silenced. This environment doesn't foster objective science but rather a self-reinforcing echo chamber.

Ultimately, the solutions promoted under the climate change banner often appear more focused on control and wealth redistribution than genuine environmental preservation. Carbon taxes, green energy mandates, and international agreements, such as the Paris Accord, place a disproportionate burden on poorer nations and individuals, while enriching corporations and governments through subsidies and compliance markets.

HYPOCRISY OF ELITES WHO PREACH CLIMATE CRISIS

If the crisis were truly existential, why do we see significant exemptions for mass polluters, including China and India, or private jet-flying elites preaching austerity for the masses? The push for net-zero policies ignores their economic devastation—skyrocketing energy costs, supply chain disruptions, and job losses—while viable alternatives, such as nuclear energy, are sidelined.

This suggests a motive that is less about saving the planet and more about exploiting fear to justify power grabs and social engineering. The climate change narrative, with its dubious science and hypocritical solutions, crumbles under scrutiny as a fabricated hoax.

THE THREAT OF CLIMATE LOCKDOWNS

One significant concern is that climate change could be leveraged to impose climate lockdowns by governments or global entities framing extreme weather events or rising CO2 levels as immediate, existential threats requiring draconian measures, much like the COVID-19 pandemic. Something global elites would most likely immediately endorse if given the opportunity.

Utilizing an authoritarian model, these might justify restricting travel, enforcing curfews, or limiting energy consumption, such as mandating reduced heating, cooling, or vehicle use, under the guise of curbing emissions.

These measures, driven by the demonic spirit of the age, could be enforced through digital tracking systems, similar to vaccine passports, monitoring individual carbon footprints via smart meters or apps. Noncompliance might result in fines, restricted access to services, or social penalties, with fear-driven narratives amplified by the media to ensure public compliance. This would mirror the lockdowns that prioritized public health over personal freedoms.

TWO IRONIC CASES OF RESEARCH SHIPS BECOMING TRAPPED IN ICE

1. A notable and ironic case involved the MS Malmö, an Arctic tour ship carrying 16 passengers, including a climate change documentary film team, which got unintentionally stuck in rapidly increasing ice on September 3, 2019, off Longyearbyen, Svalbard. As they were preparing to document the effects of global warming, they must have been surprised to be captured by that fast-growing ice. Passengers were evacuated by helicopter, leaving seven crew members to wait for Coast Guard assistance.
2. The Kronprins Haakon, a Norwegian research icebreaker, was forced to retreat in July 2019 after encountering unexpectedly thick and massive sea ice northeast of Svalbard while studying global warming and climate change effects. The ice, up to three meters thick, proved impenetrable even for its powerful design.

I encourage you, dear reader, to do your homework on climate change.[23] Read articles that offer an alternative point of view and come to your conclusions.[24]

Many of these ruling powers at work purposefully do not align with liberty, and certainly not the Bible. The policies and mechanisms marshaled through propaganda are being set up for the eventual arrival of the Antichrist.

WORLD ECONOMIC FORUM

The World Economic Forum (WEF), World Health Organization (WHO), United Nations (UN), and the push for Central Bank Digital Currencies (CBDCs) collectively pose significant risks to global sovereignty, individual freedom, and economic autonomy. The WEF, with its initiatives such as the

Great Reset, advocates for centralized control over resources and economies, often aligning with the UN, the world elites, and their agendas, which critics argue prioritize globalist policies over national interests.[25]

WORLD HEALTH ORGANIZATION

The WHO's expanding authority, seen in its proposed pandemic treaty, could enable it to impose health mandates across borders, overriding local governance and personal choice under the guise of global health security. These organizations, unelected and unaccountable to the public, foster a technocratic framework where dissent is sidelined, and policies are shaped by elite consensus rather than democratic will. Their influence risks eroding cultural identities and economic independence, as nations are pressured to conform to standardized, top-down directives.

CENTRAL BANK DIGITAL CURRENCIES

CBDCs or Central Bank Digital Currencies amplify these dangers by enabling unprecedented surveillance and control over financial systems. Unlike cash, CBDCs allow governments and central banks to track every transaction, potentially restricting purchases or freezing accounts based on behavior, as seen in China's social credit system. The WEF has championed CBDCs for their "programmability," which could let authorities limit spending on disapproved items, like fossil fuels or firearms, or impose expiry dates to force consumption.[26]

Many whistleblowers highlight fears that CBDCs, paired with AI, could create "dystopian digital prisons" or "15-minute cities," where individuals lose financial autonomy. Combined with the WEF, WHO, and UN's push for digital IDs and global governance, CBDCs could anchor a system where privacy is extinct, and compliance is enforced through economic exclusion, threatening the very foundation of free societies.

THE ***EKKLESIA*** IS THE ANSWER

Remember that no matter what the forces of darkness concoct, we, the *Ekklesia,* are here to confront it. From the small child who prays, to the elderly grandmother contending in faith for her family and nation, *greater is He who is in us than he, the spirit of antichrist, who is in the world.* With Jesus working through you, you are the dominant force in a present evil age. Nothing mentioned in this chapter can harm you or overcome the body of Christ. As long as we don't shrink back, we will win!

MY PRAYER FOR YOU

In the name of Jesus, I command whatever is coming against you to leave you. I command sickness, mental anxiety, and poverty to leave. I ask the Lord to give strength to come upon your life. I come in victory and agreement and release the full covenant of Jesus Christ over you and your situation. You're an overcomer by the blood of the Lamb and the word of your testimony and because you have lost your life for Jesus. In Jesus' name, amen.

Remember, Christ in you, the hope of glory, is a dominating force against the forces of evil.

Even on a bad day, you are anointed to be the very best there is!

It is time for you, brother and sister, to rise and be who God called you to be. This is your hour. This is your time. I bless you.

For Jesus,
Joseph Z

NOTES

Chapter One

1. IVP Bible Background commentary on 2 Kings 6:13 showing the distance of 10 miles from Dothan to Samaria.
2. Summarized Bible Commentary of 2 Kings 6:1-33 makes mention of a Siege of Samaria by Syrians.

Chapter Two

1. "Who was Nimrod in the Bible," *GotQuestions.org,* https://www.gotquestions.org/Nimrod-in-the-Bible.html.
2. Joseph Z, *The Spirit of Elijah* (Harrison House, 2025), 207.
3. https://home.cern/news/press-release/cern/stephen-hawking-tours-future-particle-physics-cern; "Sergio Bertolucci," *Wikipedia The Free Encyclopedia,* last edited August 30, 2024, https://en.wikipedia.org/wiki/Sergio_Bertolucci.
4. Lewis Page, "'Something may come through' dimensional 'doors' at LHC," *The Register,* November 6, 2009, https://www.theregister.com/2009/11/06/lhc_dimensional_portals.
5. Joel, "CERN and Bible Prophecy," *Christian Evidence,* May 31, 2019, https://www.christianevidence.net/2019/05/cern-and-bible-prophecy.html.

6. Word Study Commentary on the Greek New Testament of Revelation 6:2.
7. "Wikipedia: Wormhole," *Wikipedia The Free Encyclopedia,* last edited June 23, 2025, https://en.wikipedia.org/wiki/Wormhole.
8. "Wikipedia: Black hole," *Wikipedia The Free Encyclopedia,* last edited July 2, 2025, https://en.wikipedia.org/wiki/Black_hole.
9. Joel, "CERN and Bible Prophecy."
10. "Wikipedia: World Wide Web," *Wikipedia The Free Encyclopedia,* last edited June 30, 2025, https://en.wikipedia.org/wiki/World_Wide_Web.
11. "Wikipedia: Cernunnos," *Wikipedia The Free Encyclopedia,* last edited June 29, 2025, https://en.wikipedia.org/wiki/Cernunnos.
12. "Wikipedia: Dharmachakra," *Wikipedia The Free Encyclopedia,* last edited March 24, 2025, https://en.wikipedia.org/wiki/Dharmachakra.
13. "Discourses on an Alien Sky #13, The Bull of Heaven," *YouTube,* 2015, https://www.youtube.com/watch?v=j5O_gSguEMo.
14. "Babel: A Tower of Evidence," *Christian Evidence,* March 12, 2023, https://www.christianevidence.net/2023/03/evidence-for-tower-of-babel.html.
15. "Experiments," *CERN,* https://home.cern/science/experiments.
16. "Wikipedia: Baphomet," *Wikipedia The Free Encyclopedia,* last edited June 21, 2025, https://en.wikipedia.org/wiki/Baphomet.
17. "Wikipedia: Eye of Providence," *Wikipedia The Free Encyclopedia,* last edited May 22, 2025, https://en.wikipedia.org/wiki/Eye_of_Providence.
18. Joel, "CERN and Bible Prophecy."
19. Elon Musk, "Please let me use the CERN large hadron collider," posted on X, August 21, 2022, https://x.com/elonmusk/status/1561475238705401856?s=61.

Chapter Three

1. "Summary of the Book of 1 John," *GotQuestions,* https://www.gotquestions.org/Book-of-1-John.html.
2. Paul Harvey, "If I were the devil, I would encourage schools…." *Illinois Fraternal Order Of Police,* 1965, https://www.ilfop.org/if-i-were-the-devil-by-paul-harvey.

3. "Charles Baudelaire Quotes," *GoodReads.com*, https://www.goodreads.com/quotes/8784723-the-greatest-trick-the-devil-ever-pulled-was-convincing-the.

Chapter Four

1. Joseph Z, *Servants of Fire: Secrets of the Unseen War and Angels Fighting for You* (Harrison House Publishers, 2023), 122-128.

Chapter Five

1. Joseph Z, *Servants of Fire,* 171.
2. Joseph Z, *Servants of Fire,* 171-173.
3. Joseph Z, *Servants of Fire,* 202-204.

Chapter Seven

1. The Complete Hebrew Word Study Dictionary on Job 1:12.
2. Joseph Z, *Servants of Fire,* 20-24.

Chapter Eight

1. Joseph Z, *Servants of Fire,* 26-27.

Chapter Thirteen

1. Joseph Z. *Servants of Fire,* 29-40.
2. Joseph Z, *Servants of Fire,* 268-275.

Chapter Fourteen

1. Rick Renner, *Fallen Angels, Giants, Monsters and the World Before the Flood: How the Events of Noah's Ark and the Flood Are Relevant to the End of the Age* (Harrison House Publishers, 2024), 670.
2. "List of science-fiction authors," *WikipediaThe Free Encyclopedia,* last edited June 27, 2025, https://en.wikipedia.org/wiki/Science_fiction_authors.
3. "Vernor Vinge," *Wikipedia The Free Encyclopedia,* last edited November 19, 2024, https://en.wikipedia.org/wiki/Vernor_Vinge.
4. Ray Kurzweil, *The Singularity Is Near, When Humans Transcend Biology,* 2005.

5. Aldous Huxley, *Brave New World and Brave New World Revisited* (HarperPerennial, 2005), https://www.amazon.com/Brave-New-World-Revisited/dp/0060776099.
6. Joseph Z, *Servants of Fire,* Kindle Edition, 139-140.
7. "Project Blue Beam," *RationalWiki,* last edited May 18, 2025, https://rationalwiki.org/wiki/Project_Blue_Beam.
8. Serge Monast, *The Greatest Hoax: NASA's Project Blue Beam* (Ethos, 2024), https://www.amazon.com/Greatest-Hoax-NASAs-Project-Blue/dp/8419006823.
9. Flynn Nicholls, "What Is Project Blue Beam: Conspiracy Theory Erupts Over Drones," *Newsweek,* December 16, 2024, https://www.newsweek.com/what-project-blue-beam-conspiracy-theory-erupts-over-drones-2001051.
10. Grok Conversation, "Project Blue Beam Hologram," post on X, nd, https://x.com/i/grok/share/cJ2GrPicwztQx3Q0TAhUBJT0P.
11. "Project Blue Beam," *RationalWiki.*
12. Aidan Brophillius, *PROJECT BLUE BEAM: The Quest for a New World Order and the Rule of the Antichrist* (Audio, 2024); https://www.amazon.com/PROJECT-BLUE-BEAM-Quest-Antichrist/dp/B0CY5BM8TM.

    Joseph Sherwood, "What Is Project Blue Beam?: Everything You Need to Know About the Universal Religion Conspiracy Theory," *A Little Bit Human,* December 16, 2024, https://alittlebithuman.com/project-blue-beam-conspiracy-explained.

    J. Staas Haught, "What is Project Blue Beam? Conspiracy theory gets attention amid New Jersey drone issue," *USATODAY, NorthJersey.com,* December 16, 2024, https://www.northjersey.com/story/news/2024/12/16/donald-trump-ally-charlie-kirk-claims-drones-over-nj-are-project-blue-beam-what-is-it/77020605007.

    Abhinav Singh, ed., "Mysterious Drone Sightings Across US Linked to Project Blue Beam Conspiracy Theory," *NDTV,* December 16, 2024, https://www.ndtv.com/offbeat/mysterious-drone-sightings-across-us-linked-to-project-blue-beam-conspiracy-theory-7259650.
13. Molly Dowdeswell, October 14, 2022. "The Galli: The Cross-Dressing Cybele Cult of Priests Who Castrated Themselves," https://www.ancient-origins.net/history-ancient-traditions/galli-0017397.

14. Bob and Helga, "Trouble in Translation: 1 Timothy 2:12 & 1 Timothy 5:13-14," Apostles Warning, August 4, 2016, https://apostleswarning.wordpress.com/2016/08/04/trouble-in-translation-1-timothy-212-1-timothy-513-14:

    The cult of Cybele is not directly mentioned in the Bible. However, some biblical passages and early Christian writings reference aspects of the cult or compare it to Christian beliefs. For instance, the Apostle Paul's letter to Timothy mentions a form of asceticism that may have been influenced by the "oriental cults," including the cult of Cybele. Additionally, some early Christian writers, such as John Chrysostom, connected the practices of certain sects with the mythology of Cybele. The influence of the Cybele cult on early Christian thought and practices is a topic of discussion among scholars, but there is no direct mention of the cult in the biblical texts themselves.
15. *Conium maculatum,* known as hemlock (British English) or poison hemlock (American English), is a highly poisonous flowering plant in the carrot family Apiaceae, native to Europe and North Africa. "Wikipedia: Conium maculatum," *Wikipedia The Free Encyclopedia,* https://en.wikipedia.org/wiki/Conium_maculatum, last edited June 20, 2025.
16. Lucius Cornelius Sulla Felix (138–78 BC), commonly known as Sulla, was a Roman general and statesman of the late Roman Republic.
17. Mark Legg, "What does the Bible say about transhumanism?" *Denison Forum,* June 20, 2023, https://www.denisonforum.org/resources/bible-transhumanism.
18. Rene Ostberg, "Transhumanism," *Britannica,* June 26, 2025, https://www.britannica.com/topic/transhumanism.
19. Miquel-Angel Serra, "Human enhancement and functional diversity: Ethical concerns of emerging technologies and transhumanism," *University of Valencia,* May 11, 2021, https://www.redalyc.org/journal/5117/511769287027/html.
20. "What Is Climate Change?" *United Nations,* nd, https://www.un.org/en/climatechange/what-is-climate-change.
21. Josh Kelety, "Old video of Weather Channel co-founder fuels climate misinfo," *Associated Press,* July 24, 2022, https://apnews.com/article/fact-check-john-coleman-climate-change-176441300111.
22. Key points about the Climate Gate emails and their context:

Content of Emails:

- The emails, spanning 1996–2009, included discussions among scientists about climate data, peer review, and responses to skeptics. Phrases like "Mike's Nature trick" and "hide the decline" were highlighted by critics. The "trick" referred to a method of combining instrumental temperature data with proxy data (like tree rings) to create coherent graphs, and "hide the decline" addressed the tree-ring divergence problem, where some proxy data after the 1960s showed declining temperatures despite rising instrumental records. These were technical discussions, but skeptics misrepresented them as evidence of fraud.
- "Wiki: Climatic Research Unit email controversy," Wikipedia The Free Encyclopedia, last edited June 9, 2025, https://en.wikipedia.org/wiki/Climatic_Research_Unit_email_controversy; https://www.theguardian.com/environment/2010/jul/07/hacked-climate-emails-analysis.

Allegations and Misinterpretations:

- Skeptics, including Senator Jim Inhofe and Sarah Palin, claimed the emails showed scientists falsifying global warming evidence. For example, an email from Kevin Trenberth lamenting the inability to "account for the lack of warming" in 2008 was cited as evidence of doubt, but it reflected a discussion about short-term climate variability, not the long-term warming trend. Similarly, emails about avoiding Freedom of Information (FOI) requests or deleting correspondence raised concerns about transparency but did not indicate data fabrication.
- "Debunking Misinformation About Stolen Climate Emails in the 'Climategate' Manufactured Controversy," *Union of Concerned Scientists,* December 8, 2009, updated August 25, 2011, https://www.ucs.org/resources/debunking-misinformation-about-stolen-climate-emails.
- Andrew Revkin, "Hacked E-Mail Is New Fodder for Climate Dispute," *New York Times,* November 21, 2009, https://www.nytimes.com/2009/11/21/science/earth/21climate.html.

Investigations and Outcomes:

- Multiple independent inquiries followed, including those by the UK House of Commons, Penn State University, the University of East Anglia, and others. All cleared the scientists of misconduct, affirming that the science behind human-driven global warming remained robust. The inquiries criticized some scientists for a lack of openness with data and occasional unprofessional language but found no evidence of data manipulation or fraud. The IPCC and global temperature records were unaffected.

- Damian Carrington, "Q&A: Climategate," *The Guardian.com,* November 22, 2011, https://www.theguardian.com/environment/2010/jul/07/climate-emails-question-answer.
- Raghu Garud, et.al., "Boundaries, breaches, and bridges: The case of Climategate," ScienceDirect, February 2014, https://www.sciencedirect.com/science/article/abs/pii/S0048733313001236.

Impact and Legacy:

- The controversy fueled public distrust in climate science, amplified by media coverage and skeptic blogs. It led to harassment of scientists, with Phil Jones receiving death threats. The timing, just before the Copenhagen Summit, likely weakened momentum for global climate agreements. However, it also prompted improvements in data transparency and public engagement by climate scientists. Despite claims on X that the emails exposed a "climate scam," the scientific consensus on anthropogenic global warming has only strengthened since, with eight of the warmest years on record occurring post-2009.
- Robin McKie, "Climategate 10 years on: what lessons have we learned?" *The Guardian,* November 9, 2019, https://www.theguardian.com/theobserver/2019/nov/09/climategate-10-years-on-what-lessons-have-we-learned.
- Edward Maibach, et.al., "The legacy of climategate: undermining or revitalizing climate science and policy? *WIREs,* April 26, 2012, https://wires.onlinelibrary.wiley.com/doi/10.1002/wcc.168.
- Tony Heller, post on X, September 1, 2024, https://x.com/TonyClimate/status/1830182217907388657.

X Sentiment:

- Posts on X from 2023–2025, like those from @TonyClimate and @TomANelson, continue to cite the emails as evidence of data tampering, often focusing on specific phrases without context. These claims lack substantiation from the investigations and are not supported by the broader scientific record. Tom Nelson, post on X, April 26, 2025, https://x.com/TomANelson/status/1916076154408120454.

- Wide Awake Media, post on X, November 1, 2024, https://x.com/wideawake_media/status/1852278348287754677.
- The Climategate emails, when examined in context, reveal technical and sometimes heated discussions among scientists but do not undermine the evidence for human-driven climate change. The controversy highlights challenges in science communication and the impact of selective framing by critics.
- "What do the 'Climategate' hacked CRU emails tell us?" *Skeptical Science,* updated July 12, 2024, https://skepticalscience.com/Climategate-CRU-emails-hacked.htm.
- Fred Pearce, "The five key leaked emails from UEA's Climatic Research Unit," *The Guardian,* July 7, 2020, https://www.theguardian.com/environment/series/climate-wars-hacked-emails.

23. Joel Smalley, "Debunking The Climate Change Hoax," *Principia Scientific International,* May 28, 2024, https://principia-scientific.com/debunking-the-climate-change-hoax.
24. Jonathan Gault, "Simple Facts Expose The Climate Change Hoax," *American Thinker,* October 25, 2024, https://www.americanthinker.com/articles/2024/10/simple_facts_expose_the_climate_change_hoax.html.
25. World Economic Forum defined by Grok3 on X.
26. E.J. Antoni and Peter St. Onge, "Pushers of Central Bank Digital Currencies Are the Most Terrifying of Villains," *The Heritage Foundation,* July 20, 2023, https://www.heritage.org/monetary-policy/commentary/pushers-central-bank-digital-currencies-are-the-most-terrifying-villains.

ABOUT JOSEPH Z

Joseph Z is an author, broadcaster, and international prophetic voice. He and his wife, Heather, have dedicated their lives to preaching the gospel and building lives by the Voice of God; as a result, they have built Bible schools, churches, and prophetic conferences in the United States and worldwide. Their daily broadcast currently reaches a global audience, emphasizing prophetic events. Additionally, they are the founders of Joseph Z Ministries, a media and conference-based ministry with offices and production studios located in Colorado.

For Further Information

If you would like prayer or further information about Joseph Z Ministries, please call our offices at (719) 257-8050 or visit JosephZ.com/contact.

Visit JosephZ.com for additional materials.